This Just In:

A Zombie Novel

Sometimes truth is stranger than fiction

Lisa Fedel

Pro -tip: don't die

Lisa Fedel

Copyright Page

I have a soft spot in my heart for the zombies.

— **GEORGE A. ROMERO**

Dedication

This book is dedicated to Ally Agic, who liked it from the first draft.

Prologue

"Should we be concerned that Adrian only ended up living one town away from us?" David asked his wife, Georgia, during a Sunday morning golf outing. Georgia never participated in the sport, and always just ended up hauling all of the gear. She didn't particularly enjoy these trips for a multitude of reasons, the least of which was not that David always found a reason to be stressed. The worst days were the times he stressed about their daughter.

Allowing the bag of golf clubs to fall to the ground so David could get the club he needed, Georgia replied that it wasn't strictly Adrian's decision to move to Springfield, it was just where she'd gotten offered a job. Technically, Adrian never wanted to stay in Ohio for her life (she'd made a point to choose a college in Michigan), but after she was offered a position at News Sun directly out of college, she wasn't going to turn the job down.

"I guess," David agreed with a shrug, hitting the golf ball with his club. He watched as it flew several yards away, landing directly into the river he was trying to avoid. "Damn." This normally would not be such an inconvenience, but this particular river led into a newly built chemical treatment plant. Townspeople were mad, but the town argued that it was for the greater good. Either way, David waded into the shallow water containing his golf ball to continue the game. He took a moment, noticing the amount of fish darting around, crowding the ball. They swam away as he reached downward and plucked it out, but he didn't enjoy the fact that they'd been that close to his lucky ball.

Georgia had always enjoyed going to the beach when she was young, mainly because she liked to splash in the water and watch the fish all swim away. She was disappointed that the fish in this pond weren't the small whitings she liked to harass, but rather bigger fish the size of the ones in the tanks at fancy Chinese restaurants. On top of that, the fish didn't really seem to care he was in the water until he had reached down. She wished he would have just decided to leave the ball in the water and either use a different ball or go home, but there were still two holes to play through, and it was a pretty nice day out. Sundays always involved either coming to this golf course, or going to a cute mini golf course that Georgia didn't mind quite as much as the long days spent here. That being said, however, her husband was young at heart and liked to pose for photos with all of the different statues along the mini golf course, which always meant they stayed at that course for the same amount of time as they would this regular golf course.

"So we're going to finish the course, then?" she muttered, hoping he'd pick up on her desire to leave.

Glancing at the ball now sitting on the sand, David made a decision. "I'm feeling kind of run down, honestly, and even though I can tell *you're* having an excellent time, we should probably pack up and go home."

4

Ch. 1
The Front Page

"There is change in the air. Along with the upcoming change of seasons, the bug population has decreased significantly," the head news anchor reported on Saturday morning. Summer was ending and fall was upon the people of Springfield, Ohio, but nobody took much notice to the report of the bugs.

Perpetually curious about what was going on in the world, Adrian Chase always tuned to the WHIO news channel before going to work. She turned it off directly after this report. If anything worth noting was going on, she'd know once she got to her job at the town's other reporting network, News Sun. She was one of three copyeditors, fact checking the major stories—though it wasn't often that she found any type of error. In a town like Springfield, the stories they covered tended to be small: a sports team went against another sports team and won, a school is putting on some sort of concert, there's been talk about a store moving to another location, and similar news pertaining to just the townspeople. Working as the fact checker she was also often asked if something was worth reporting, and she made sure they never reported the dull stories WHIO tended to cover.

She always left the house precisely eleven minutes before work, and it was coming up to the thirteen minute mark. Her husband, Charlie Baker, who owned a Star Trek themed coffee shop called That Nebula (anybody who knew the reference got an extra espresso for free), was not awake yet. She didn't want to wake him up to say goodbye this morning. The two of them had a rule: if she knew she'd be staying late at the office one night, or Charlie knew he would be late at the coffee shop interviewing potential new employees, or closing by himself, they would wake each other up. It didn't seem like a big deal today. The whole thing was a tricky business: they had a silent agreement never to wake one another up if it seemed redundant, and Adrian decided that since they'd be going to a family picnic that evening, Charlie could continue his slumber.

Adrian showed up early for work every day for one reason: she could go to various news websites and read about what was going on in the world. She'd always enjoyed reading the news, and loved that she had a job in which there was actually logical reasoning for her to do so. The internet connectivity she had at work was much better than what she had at her house, and the company didn't care how much extra time she spent in the office, so long as they continued only paying per article as opposed to by the hour. There usually wasn't even anything for her to do when she first arrived, even if she *did* show up at 9:00 instead of 8:51.

On the way out of the house, she grabbed the book she was currently reading off of the table. It never hurt to have spare reading material for those times in the day that there wasn't anything interesting on the news sites, and she was rereading one of her favorites, anyway. It was a horror novel that was slightly comedic, and the kind of book that she loved to go back to at certain times in her life. Charlie had given it to her on their first date, as he wanted to give her something but wanted to avoid the cliche of flowers or chocolates.

It was a book about zombies, but seemed more up his alley than hers, so she had put off reading it for a while. Eventually, she read it when she was in the hospital for a sleep study, as she had some unknown condition that kept her body from getting the effect of a full night's sleep, no matter how many hours she slept or what state of sleep she was in for that time. The test was horrible: she was plugged into a bunch of annoyingly loud and uncomfortable machines, there were tubes in her nose, and she couldn't even fathom how she was going to be able to be monitored as "sleeping normally" when she was set up like this. From then on out, any time she had to have one of these tests, she would bring this book to sort of cheer her up.

She knew it was ironic.

The town looked completely as she'd always known it on the way to work: the YMCA building with the painting advertising a long since past Lillian and Dorthy Gish performance, the many abandoned buildings on the outskirts of town, and all of the small houses in the neighborhoods she drove by until ending up at the parking lot of News Sun building, already filled up with cars of the reporters, manager and janitors who she liked to imagine never actually left. With a sigh, she pulled her car out of the lot and parked across the street as usual. Even though parking in the other lot wasn't anything new for her and the company would reimburse the $5 all day parking fee, she always got excited when she managed to get a space in her building's parking lot.

She walked across the street and opened the glass door of the building which had last received the Community Beautification Award in 1989. She was greeted in the normal fashion by Karen the receptionist (a young blonde woman, already bored of life and her job), and headed to her office to find she only had one assignment so far today: a fact check on the story they were doing on a soccer game where (the note read) "some serious shit had gone down." The 24 hour news cycle was not a myth, but at her job, a small assignment such as this one was fairly common in the morning. No news here was ever "breaking" or involved anything gruesome, but it was a steady job, and it paid the bills. Unfortunately, while she was the person to go to if you wanted information on truth versus fiction, she was not one to know how to find out about sports. The man she knew would have information on this subject was another copyeditor named Hank Walker, who followed anything and everything sports. He'd originally wanted to be in the journalism business as a big sports reporter on television, but that came to an end after an accident in high school. A major athlete for the majority of his life, it was a sports injury that completely changed his life in the worst possible way: brain damage that prevented his ability to ever play another game. When he was in high school, there was a soccer game in which a wayward ball hit him, causing him to fall forward and hit his head with such force that his brain got jolted enough to become scarred and cause him some serious medical issues. It originally got misdiagnosed as a concussion when it was actually much more severe than that. By the time the doctors realized how bad he truly had been injured, it was too late to do anything about it.

Adrian picked up her office phone and dialed the local sports nerd, who picked up on the first ring.

"What's up?" he asked, always the casual employee. Unable to get the job he had wanted, he never acted with the air of professionalism expected of those who had the job that they had always planned on getting. Nobody really expected him to, either.

"We're doing a story about the soccer game," she replied. "How would I do the fact check?" After a moment, Hank admitted, "If we're doing a story on what I think, there's really not a lot to check because nobody knows what exactly happened, just that some of the members of the opposing team started acting rather strangely." He paused. "I don't know what happened to those people afterward, but they've generally been blaming the opposing team, saying that they did something to cause the events but it's not like it matters anyway, the team with the sick people ended up winning." There was also a reason Hank couldn't write for the paper: since he never fully found a way to recover from his brain trauma, he tended to talk in run on sentences. He had the ability to think through how a sentence should sound, but every time he'd attempted writing articles, it took him several more hours than it would a person without brain damage, still never read that well, and left him with a splitting headache that he ended up at urgent care to get resolved.

"I'll call Nathan," Adrian said, aside. "Thanks for the advice, anyway."

"I don't think he's in yet," Hank warned her. Then he laughed, stating, "I know he'll be here eventually; he never misses the potluck." Nathan was the only one who enjoyed the company potluck, which was to take place in a short while when the majority of the employees would normally split for lunch. It was always an interesting assortment of food; there were folks there who were on a gluten free diet, lactose intolerant, even a guy who was triggered by the smell of Alfredo sauce. And one vegan. Adrian would usually just bring a dessert; this year it was a pan of brownies that she'd made. She put the phone back in its cradle, deciding that it would make more sense to just catch Nathan at the potluck. As the boss, he tended not to do too well if he was interrupted from something he was working on, but was always in a good mood at company events. The addition of food helped as well.

12

Ch. 2
Almost Famous

With nothing to do but a desire to at least *feel* productive, Adrian decided to check out the background of the news story she'd started listening to at home, in case News Sun would be covering it as well. It became apparent very quickly that she didn't have the information she needed to know if there was any meat to the story; she'd turned it off before finding out any of the information. Her curiosity came from a purely journalistic point of view: it had mentioned "bugs" as a general term, which could mean the things in general or a specific one. Once she'd decided there was nothing to do about the bug story, she pulled out her book and started reading again.

There were few things Adrian Chase liked more than reading a good zombie novel. Unfortunately for Hank Walker, while he knew this in theory, he did not know that she happened to be a page and a half away from her favorite gruesome part of this particular one at the moment he decided to stop by for a visit.

"Dammit, Hank," Adrian said, setting her book down as she tried to connect with the real world once again after being intensely startled by his knock.

"Nice to see you too, Adrian," he said in a borderline sarcastic tone, completely unfazed as he invited himself in and sat on the chair she had set by the wall. His stopping by wasn't an oddity (in fact he was the only one who tended to visit), but today's visit was a bit less than welcome.

"Sorry," she apologized, suddenly realizing how rude she had unintentionally been to her only friend at work. They were not only good friends, but Hank was just a great person in general. Although he couldn't do much to help himself and his own problems, he always did everything he could to make sure everyone else had what they needed. "I was reading. You know me, and I was just getting to the good part and, well, zombies are *scary*. I was really there in the action for a minute."

"No biggie," Hank replied with a shrug. He knew he wasn't the first one you'd want to see if you were reading a scary book. His sudden appearance had not only shock value, but he had a wicked scar extending diagonally across his face. The accident that ruined his future in sports reporting not only gave him brain damage, but this scar also. But he knew Adrian well and was not new to these outbursts.

"So what's up?" she said, bringing her chair

closer to her desk and folding her hands.

"Just life," Hank replied with an indifferent shrug. Hank had a certain way of talking about how he was doing. 'Just life' was always a code for his complete inability to even approach Lucy, the female reporter he was in love with, due to his own insecurities about how he looked. He'd never had an actual conversation with her, but he was friends with her on Facebook, so he knew a bit about her personal life. She loved animals: she was a vegan as well as a foster mom, accepting stray dogs into her house, making sure they were well taken care of and socialized before adopting them out so they didn't have to go to the Humane Society where they would be kept in crates.

As many times as Adrian and others had assured him that he was much more than the scar that stretched across his face, she knew he had never done anything to try to tell Lucy how he felt. He had a good sense of humor, a bad (or good, depending on who you ask) habit of correcting people's grammar, and was an all around good person. "Did you ever get the information on the sporting event?"

"Nah," she answered. "Since it's such a small thing and such a weird thing, I'm putting it off until I know for sure what's going on. I feel like we might not even end up reporting on it anyway, with so many other things going on right now." This was a joke among the two: since they worked in a town where so few things ever happened, there were never any big other things.

"It sucks that that's all they assigned you so

far," Hank told her. "You're just going to be stuck here with nothing to do." He glanced at the door. "I could easily check with the others and see if they need help, so you're not *entirely* bored."

"Twenty four hour news cycle," she muttered, checking her inbox to see if anyone had sent her another assignment. She really didn't care to put any extra stress on him. Seeing nothing there, she had to remind herself that the reason she had chosen to work for a reporting company was the fact that allegedly there would always be some news coming in, something that needed to be done. Such had not been the case so far for News Sun. Suddenly remembering what WHIO had reported, however, she blurted, "Hey do you know if we're doing anything about bugs?"

"Bugs?" Hank echoed. "I didn't get anything about them, but maybe one of the others did, you might wanna ask Karl." It made sense that he wouldn't have any more information than she did, as his position was essentially the same as hers. Karl Aster, the head nighttime news reporter, however, *would* be the guy to ask. He wasn't the nicest guy in the world, though. Still, she assumed it was on the lower end of importance, sure she'd know by the time the news was on that night.

"Fair enough," Adrian said with a shrug. "Channel 7"—where Adrian worked nobody dared speak the actual name of the network—"was reporting something about bugs this morning, and I just wondered if there was anything to it." Hank assured her it was nothing to worry about, then signaled to the book on her desk, which she had left as bait. He completely took said bait, asking her about why she was reading it. He'd never seen her reading it before, but knowing this woman, it was safe to assume it was *re*read, and she knew each and every little detail about it: the relationships between the characters, the roles they all played in one another's lives, and who survived until the end.

Adrian answered that she liked it because it had many literary elements but still managed to be intensely gruesome, going into extreme detail about how the zombies killed and were killed. It wasn't normal workplace conversation, but Adrian never minded talking about zombies with someone she got along with well.

"So, '*just life*'," Adrian said after giving him a complete rundown of the book. "She's still out of reach for you?"

"It just... it just kills me, you know?" Hank said. "What would my life be like without this scar: would I be hot, would I look like a dork (I mean, I do wear glasses), would I even have the guts to go talk to her?"

"I can see how that would upset you," Adrian said with a nod, still hating how vague he always was about his issues. She was completely open to him talking about his problems and trying to help him out, but she knew he never would. "But didn't your girlfriend in high school not even care?"

"Jennifer knew me before the scar," Hank answered, "I was actually someone back then: I was a jock, totally on my way to becoming a big sports news reporter, and now look at me: I have an office in a little corner of the building doing work that no non-Journalism student even knows goes on in a reporting office while she's the day time news reporter who *everybody* knows about. And Jennifer is officially done with me. Just called me: she's actually getting married, our little thing we had going? It's done now. She's absolutely done seeing me." So not 'just life'. 'Just life' and 'the usual'.

"But what about your medical things?" Adrian asked, wanting to help him feel better. "Is she still going to be there for that?"

"She is, but she isn't very happy about it," he deadpanned. "Neither is her fiancé. And here's the clincher: if I do have one of my episodes during those events? She won't help me feel better after the fact, she thinks that her having been there will be enough." As much as Adrian hated herself for acknowledging the fact, both parties had valid points: the two had stayed close after their high school break up, solely because of Hank's illness. She was always there in whatever manner he needed. He'd never take advantage of her kindness, but she'd been there for him, coming up on eight years now. And if she was getting married, her fiancé was obviously not okay with Hank not only being part of her life, but also the fact that Hank and Jennifer's physical relationship had never ended.

19

Ch. 3
Network

The conversation they were having distracted her from the fact that her day was going so slowly, *and* made them late to the potluck. Double bonus.

"Should we even go?" Adrian asked, giving Hank an automatic out since he was never at his best after spending any amount of time talking about his accident.

"We kind of have to," Hank reminded her. "Nathan's up there and there's food."

"True," she agreed getting up out of her chair. "Let's just go now." As much of a pain as the potluck was, Hank was right, and she was starting to get hungry.

"I'll be up in a bit," Hank said, watching her leave the room, "technically I wasn't supposed to have left my office yet today, but I was upset and I knew you were here, but if we show up together then Nathan is bound to know I wasn't doing what I was supposed to be doing. I've been told I'm easy to read."

"You are, but that plan works," Adrian said, fully aware that the real reason he didn't want to leave yet was that he was worried about running into Lucy. His mind couldn't exactly comprehend that if she was going to be there it didn't matter if he showed up first, she did or both at the same time. The brain damage he'd gotten had really messed up his life. She understood this and didn't try to make him see things in a way he couldn't.

Hank watched Adrian leave the office, wishing he had the ability to recover mentally faster than he knew he could. Lucy was a beautiful, caring woman, and she would probably be able to handle his issues, but he couldn't handle the possibility that she might not be understanding about it. Even if she was, he really didn't want to put her through the process of having to learn about everything he needed. He couldn't bring himself to even consider putting her through that, as he could barely manage it himself. He took a plethora of medication every morning to be able to function, stay semi-level headed when he had a problem in life, and try to minimize his seizures. He'd been diagnosed with epilepsy far later than he should have, meaning the episodes could just barely be controlled by medication. Really, all the pills did was keep him from needing to be hospitalized when he had the problems, but he still had severe dizzy spells and threw up often. If he and Lucy ended up getting serious, she would have to adjust to a lot of differences in a life that, at least from the outside, seemed perfect. Maybe some day it wouldn't seem as perfect as it appeared, but for now, it looked like there were no worries in her life aside from how sad she was about leaving her foster dogs when she spent the day at work.

When Adrian got to the conference room that was featuring today's picnic, she was genuinely startled by how crowded the room had become. It was so unexpected, in fact, that she was suddenly reminded of the tiny packed rooms she used to have to sit in while the doctors and her parents discussed what was the best action to take for her sleeping issues: herself in an uncomfortable hospital bed, still hooked up to machines to monitor her breathing and brain rhythms during the night, an IV painfully located in her hand or arm, her parents sitting in poorly upholstered chairs by the window, her GP accompanied by enough sleep specialists to make the room too crowded to feel right, and her stomach churning knowing they wouldn't have any *new* information.

To distract herself from these awful memories, she scanned the room, looking for familiar friendly faces. She saw Karl Aster, the handsome (if cocky) night time news reporter, standing at a table with an outdated news article tablecloth, laughing about something either he or Nancy, the red haired intern-turned-on-call-news-reporter, had said.

Adrian had never gotten close with Karl, and couldn't really understand how anybody who did, could. All she knew was that any time he was upset about needing to repeat himself multiple times, he would become irrationally angry and lash out, trying to make others feel as bad as he did.

She couldn't remember if she'd ever experienced this for herself, but she knew this because he'd done it plenty of times to Hank when he'd used sentences that were too long for him to understand. Hank got it a lot. Nancy wasn't as problematic as Karl, but was the only openly gay employee, and while Adrian didn't have an issue with it, the intern talked about it a lot. Having gotten the speech multiple times, Adrian wasn't in the mood for it at the moment. Truth be told, Nancy was stunningly beautiful, but Adrian was both married, and not interested in women. She wasn't really friends with either of them since they worked so far apart and never really spoke to each other unless it was work related, so she kept looking.

Naturally, Trevor Walsh, the company's head IT guy, was there as a joke. No surprise there: it was a tradition established early on from these picnics which were technically meant to be just for the people who worked reporting somehow, but he had absent-mindedly shown up one day and nobody informed him until the picnic was over that he really wasn't allowed. He was fun, but still not a person she wanted to talk to.

She didn't see the counselor, Raleigh, yet, but had to assume she was having an appointment with someone. Raleigh was a seemingly normal person, if a bit bothersome at times, but could also be a bit...

the best way of saying it is "unique". After seeing the therapist a few times for things that were going on in her life, Adrian figured out what had gotten Raleigh interested in being a therapist: she found the human mind fascinating. This came from her interest in serial killers, which is probably why she had only landed a job working at the small news company in a tiny town. She did keep a special watch on Hank, though, knowing the amount of serial killers who turned out that way due to some sort of brain damage, be it mental instability, concussion or an actual traumatic brain injury.

The only other person she did not see was Linda, the woman who organized the paper, figuring out which articles went into which section, and making sure it all looked nice. People's reasons for having the job they had were interesting to learn about: Hank was an editor because it was the only thing he could realistically still do with his disability, Karl was a reporter because he had the kind of presence that made people pay attention to him, Adrian was in her job because she'd always had fun finding errors when she was just reading books. And Linda was in her position because she loved fonts. Picking them, identifying them on billboards, but especially figuring out when they were used incorrectly on the other paper's reports.

She realized, embarrassingly late, that the other editor, Nick, was there. His job on the paper was arguably the least interesting: he checked punctuation and spelling, and made sure the articles conformed to the house style. He basically worked as spellcheck. He'd been hired since there were so many strange words in reporting that a computer would try to correct, which would just be annoying for someone who already had his or her own job to have to deal with. Anyway, another person having a job was always nice.

Nick was a weird guy, though: he enjoyed chaos and things going awry. He tended to blame this on the fact that he "never had a chance to be normal", given that his full name was Nicholas Nicholas. He couldn't really forgive his parents for giving him a weird name like that, so he embraced the strangeness of it all. Adrian knew enough about Star Trek through her husband to often compare Nick to Q from *Star Trek: The Next Generation*. Charlie had a drink titled Q's Favorite, which was a shot of espresso. Or, if you wanted multiple shots, you would order a Q2, then specify how many shots you would like.

Thinking perhaps she wouldn't want to talk to anyone until Hank was there, she was stuck thinking about how crowded it was and uncomfortable she felt. It reminded her of a very specific incident that had occurred back when she was about twelve years old. After yet another test, she had not slept at all the night before and could hardly stay awake, even with the large sugary mint flavored mocha her mother had allowed her to have for this occasion. Next to the exhaustion she had felt and the bitter taste of coffee, all she remembered was again getting the awful news that the doctors "honestly did not know what was wrong with her sleep patterns" and perhaps she should "just be glad that although always morbidly exhausted, at least she was healthy" (an exact quote that is kind of hard to forget).

Even after she'd spent that long night watching the cheesy horror films she enjoyed (such as those written in the sixties and horror comedies) this news was the worst thing she had ever experienced. It was one thing to know you have trouble getting restful sleep, but to know that plus being informed that the doctors didn't know how to help her was genuinely crushing. She'd been getting by on the knowledge that they hadn't done any testing yet, but now that her brain waves had been analyzed and had apparently showed nothing was too much for her to handle.

Admittedly, it was awesome that she'd stayed up all night watching what she loved (she'd always loved things that made her skin crawl), but this news was a different kind of horror: it *was* skin crawling, but it was real. Real life horror is different from watching a scripted thing played out by attractive actors.

"I thought doctors were supposed to be smart," she had groused once the three of them had gotten into the car after the meeting.

"Adrian, dear, we knew this wasn't going to be an easy experience for any of us," her father had said, reaching out and squeezing her hand. "And it was just one doctor's opinion: there are more out there."

"That's what you said last time," she muttered angrily, wishing her life were as simple as the teenagers' in the movies she'd just watched. She spent the entire day feeling awful, only beginning to feel better when she tried once again to go to sleep, knowing the next day was a Saturday and that she had zero responsibilities and would be allowed to sleep in as long as she wanted.

"Are you alright?" Nathan asked, interrupting her reverie and suddenly at her side. She jumped, noting that he was holding a large coffee which (judging by the amount of whipped cream on top) was much like the one she'd just been thinking about.

"You get that from Charlie's?" she asked, noting the insignia on to the drink in his hand (a purposefully crudely drawn space ship). He grinned.

"Yep," he replied. "Nothing there Lucy could have, though. There's actual *cow's milk* in it and whipped cream on top." That's right; people always forgot that Nathan and Lucy had a *similar* restriction on what they could and couldn't consume, but Nathan was allowed to have eggs and milk. He was a vegetarian, meaning he didn't eat meat, but Lucy was a vegan, which meant no animal by-products whatsoever. Why she even came to the potluck was beyond everyone's understanding.

"Anyway, Chase, I didn't see what you brought." Having been so concerned with giving Hank some space, she had foolishly left the pan of brownies in her office, so she excused herself to her office to get it.

Although it was a walk she had taken countless times, and in fact a repeat (if backwards) of what she had done not ten minutes ago, a sense of being out of place washed over her as she returned to her room. She blamed the feeling on everybody else being down a floor eating food. And she was pretty sure that about three people hadn't shown up to work. The question there was whether this was because of an illness, or a desire to not be at the office. It was no secret that this building did not hold the world's greatest employees.

She picked up her pace and got to her office, grabbed the brownies, and hurried back up, this time not waiting for the elevator but taking the stairs instead.

She passed a few people on the way back, which somehow made the situation even more creepy; a deserted hallway occupied by her and only one other person did not do anything to soothe her nerves. It was reminiscent of cars driving behind her when she was the only one on the road. She reminded herself that she just read a lot of creepy stories and her subconscious was trying to put her into one of those novels. There was nothing to be worried about. She didn't see Hank on the way there or back, but he wasn't in the office when she'd gotten the brownies, so figured he must have used a different route than the one she was on.

He'd probably taken the elevator.

28

Ch. 4
Nothing But the Truth

After returning to the potluck and setting her tray on the table, she noticed Lucy Marion approaching the table and grabbing a hamburger. That was weird; it was very well known around the office that Lucy was a vegan.

That's odd, she thought. *But Lucy must be feeling better.* She'd been out for a while, saying she felt under the weather, although Adrian couldn't help but suspect she was just tired of showing up and finding out how small the stories were; a situation the on-call reporter (technically intern, Nancy) never much seemed to mind.

After a moment, Adrian realized Lucy might not have known what she had done, and walked up to the reporter. It had always seemed like a vegan accidentally eating meat would scrunch his or her face up and throw the rest of it out.

Lucy was smiling, and took a second large

bite, grabbing another burger that she clearly planned to eat once she finished the one she had. Adrian had tried vegan patties enough times to know that the texture, taste, and flavor between a beef burger and a veggie burger aren't hard to notice. Lucy knew what was currently in her mouth.

Perhaps she'd been sick because she wasn't getting enough protein, so her doctor had forced her to change her diet? And she was happy because eating meat is far superior to eating imitation meat? There had to be some explanation for this woman's sudden change.

Adrian could only imagine the bliss this vegan was in, having meat for the first time in six years. Nevertheless, she appeared to be having a special moment with the food, so Adrian slowly backed off, deciding that talking to Nathan about her assignment would be her next best thing. She had no problem finding him, already at the dessert table helping himself to a little bit of everything he *could* eat: his plate was packed with jello, various flavors of pudding, and (Adrian noticed with no small amount of pride) 3 of the brownies she had made. As the only vegetarian working at the company, he must have ignored the table that had the food, and would probably care how Lucy was acting. But Adrian was only concerned about what she needed to do for work.

"I know this is meant to be a casual picnic event, but I have a work related question," Adrian said to Nathan who was mid chew. He swallowed and asked what the issue was.

"It's just... I don't think there's any way to fact check something if literally nobody knows what happened. You know I don't know how to handle sports things as it is, but something like this? I talked to Hank, and even he seemed in the dark." He explained that the only thing he was asking for was confirmation that the events had occurred, and it wasn't just something somebody had staged. If it was just a flash mob type of event, there was no reason to report it, unless it was about the acting group that set it up.

So just another of the dull assignments that nobody else wanted to do. The company always managed to disguise those jobs as something that was "best fit for Adrian". Yes, she was in charge of making sure all of the stories were true, but this didn't feel like editor level stuff here. Relieved she didn't have to do anything that actually related to sports, she assured him that she would contact the manager of the team once she left the picnic.

"So, Hank said you were late today," Adrian mentioned, mainly because this meant that he also had to park in the spare lot. She liked that.

It wasn't like Nathan to be late; around the office, he was the one who was always on time. A day had never passed in which he didn't show up for work fifteen minutes early, if not more. Honestly, Adrian was shocked that nobody had called someone about the fact that Nathan was late. This occurrence was so unheard of that for all they knew, he may have gotten seriously injured at home or on the way to the office.

"I woke up late," Nathan replied with a shrug. "I had a bad allergic reaction last night so it was difficult to fall asleep. When my alarm went off this morning, I lost track of how many times I hit the snooze button."

"Today is just a weird day," Adrian muttered to herself.

Seemingly out of nowhere, Hank appeared, saying, "Did you get a load of Lucy today?" Already on edge, Adrian jumped. "She just ate like two cheeseburgers."

"You *would* be the one to mention that," Adrian teased. After a beat, she realized what Lucy's actions would mean in the long-run. It's one thing for a vegan to eat, like, one meatball, but one of Nancy's special giant burgers stuffed with cheese? Lucy was about to get incredibly ill.

Cautiously, she walked over to Lucy to ask how she was feeling. The reporter simply shrugged as if she hadn't just ruined the diet she'd had for the past six years of her life. She was a very proud vegan, always going on about how long she'd been on the diet, how life was without the consumption of any animal product, and why others should do the same as her. She liked to talk about not only the treatment of animals in factories, but also the lack of clean living space for them and how much air pollution went on when the meat was shipped from where it was prepared to the stores where it would be sold.

There were books very cleverly displayed in her office about these topics.

"Well why the sudden change of heart?"

Adrian tried, her inner reporter kicking in. Again all she got was a shrug, this time accompanied by a disgusted look before Lucy picked up yet *another* burger. Since she clearly didn't want to talk about it, Adrian decided to stop thinking about it and enjoy some of the food herself. She grabbed a plate and filled it with a little of everything: a cheeseburger Lucy clearly wanted to eat, some of the jello Nathan had been enjoying, and various sides brought by various people with dietary restrictions.

She sat to begin her meal and was barely a few bites in when Lucy collapsed onto the ground, unconscious. Leaving the plate on the chair next to her, Adrian went to help, all thoughts of peculiar behavior out of her head.

So not exactly the negative effect I had worried about, but still something. Unfortunately Adrian was not trained in first aid and did not know how to handle this situation. Her stress earlier had come from the possibility of Lucy throwing up, or having some sort of digestive issue later on.

She sat next to the unconscious reporter, weighing her options: find someone who could perform CPR, try to make Lucy throw up to rid her body of all the food she just ate, or assume she was going to be okay and leave her there. She checked Lucy's pulse to find it beating intermittently every five seconds or so. As a simple newspaper editor, she went to find someone who might have a better idea about what to do.

Finding somebody who could help with Lucy's problem proved to be more difficult than she had imagined. She couldn't think of anyone who was particularly proficient in the knowledge of medical emergencies, but figured Nathan might have an idea; being the boss he might be prepared for a situation like this one. And anyway, his diet was about the closest to hers as anyone else who worked for the company.

His advice was not to do anything, assuring her that the situation was bound to work itself out. As bad as she felt about that, she *was* incredibly hungry and there was a plate of food waiting for her where she would have a clear view of Lucy.

When she'd finished about half of the food on her plate, she saw Lucy stirring. The reporter then sat up, stood, and began walking around the room. It seemed random; she wasn't walking toward anything or anybody in particular. It was weird. In the end, she just left the room. Adrian shrugged, figuring it had taken a lot out of her to pass out, and went on with her meal.

Adrian eventually decided that she was through with the sad excuse for a party and that she wanted to return to her office. Granted, she still probably only had the one task, but these potlucks were always the same incredibly boring thing and she wasn't feeling very comfortable at the moment. She'd feel better in her office, where she could at least put on some music to distract herself.

She said bye to Nathan and Hank, stepped out into the hall, and called her husband so she had something to focus on other than her growing sense of unease. He opened the store late on Saturdays, so he'd probably be home for about two more hours.

"Hey," he answered, not picking up until the third ring.

"Charlie?" Adrian said. "Hey how are you?" She began walking to the stairwell, keeping an eye out for Lucy, in case she needed help.

"I'm good, but you don't sound great," he replied. "What's going on?"

"I just feel like today's been weird. Not a lot has happened, but somebody just passed out and then just left the room. Nobody knows where she is and I seem to be the only one who's worried. But then, it probably doesn't help that I was rereading my favorite book." He still wasn't convinced the book wasn't just her favorite because he'd gifted it to her, but he appreciated any time she said that.

"Honey you know you've always been the kind to blow things out of proportion," Charlie reminded her. "She was probably dehydrated and went to get something to drink once she was conscious again. If what you've complained about is true, those parties only have sugary drinks, and she would have needed water."

Adrian sighed, ashamed of herself, and a bit embarrassed. "You're right. I always look for the worst case scenario, and although I don't have a scenario in my mind, I know there's really no reason to worry."

She'd said this more to convince herself than because she believed it, but any and all embarrassment of her actions disappeared when she turned the next corner to find what she never realized was her biggest fear: the very reporter she had been worrying about, gnawing on the leg of a freshly killed corpse.

It was impossible to believe that just yesterday this person had been bragging about going out to celebrate her six years of veganism. What once had been Lucy looked up at Adrian, its cloudy eyes probably not even registering that they knew each other. The new Lucy stared, blood running from her mouth down her neck and covering her hands. The stench of death in the hallway was surprising as this kill had clearly only happened moments ago, judging by the moist puddle of blood on the carpet next to her. Adrian accidentally caught a glimpse of the corpse's face, and recognized it as a reporter she had walked by not even an hour ago: another intern, but one who was mostly only asked to fetch coffee and food.

Adrian stood, trying to process what she was seeing. It was so out of the ordinary that she struggled to believe what was happening even though it was right in front of her: surely none of this was real and she was on some stupid prank show that would drag this out for minutes that would seem to be hours until some celebrity comes out from another room and tells her all of this was scripted, right?

On the off-chance that none of this was scripted and that this *was* actually happening, Adrian turned and rushed to the stairs, hoping Lucy's brain did not function well enough to climb the stairs or know how the elevator worked. She had to get to the others and warn them about the danger. Her arms pumped as she moved faster than she knew she was capable of doing as she rushed back to the potluck to warn the others.

Ch. 5
The Pelican Brief

In no way did Adrian actually want to go back to the conference room holding the potluck. If there was a member of the company who had turned into a zombie in the hallway and a group of people in the conference room, there were almost certainly zombies in that room as well.

Pushing the negativity out of her mind as best she could, Adrian focused on something that had happened in the room that she was on her way back to: the day she got a promotion as well as a proposal.

After moving to Ohio for this job, Charlie (who was just her boyfriend at the time) moved with her, explaining that Springfield seemed like exactly the kind of place that he could open his themed coffee shop. This was partially true, but he was also planning on proposing to her when she was at work, and had been working for a while with Nathan in order to set this up.

Adrian was still fairly new to News Sun at the time, but she was a good worker. Charlie spent several months conversing with Nathan, organizing what was set to be a celebration for a promotion Adrian would be getting, but was more realistically going to be when Charlie asked Adrian to marry him. She absolutely had not expected to see Charlie standing right at the door of the conference room that day, and panicked a little bit, thinking that Nathan was going to yell at them. Before she had a chance to voice this concern, he, Charlie, was getting on one knee and asking her to marry him. It was one of the best moments of her life, and definitely a better memory than what she'd just seen in the hall.

There was no way Adrian was going to get up on a chair and announce what she had just witnessed. If she'd learned anything from what she'd seen, it was that zombies being real is something one should be eased into. With this realization, she decided to approach Raleigh with a topic the therapist knew quite a lot about.

"There were some serial killers who cannibalized their victims, right?" Adrian asked the therapist, who was standing off to the side, alone. "That wasn't just a Donner party thing?"

"Technically there's no recorded proof that the Donner party ate humans, but they did eat the animals who had come along, being how scarce supplies were," Raleigh said absently. "But if you want to talk murderers, Jeffrey Dahmer admitted to eating his victim's thighs, hearts and organs, Andrei Chikatilo lured his victims into the woods to murder and cannibalize them, uh, Albert Fish cooked and ate a little girl over the course of nine days..." Realizing she had just spouted off information on three distinct serial killers, Raleigh inquired, "Why are you asking me this?"

"So you're saying they all had a long, drawn out thing, right? They wouldn't, oh say, attack a coworker in the hallway and devour their flesh in public?"

"Not really enjoying the potluck, are we?" Raleigh observed. Trying to maintain her professional attitude, however, she asked Adrian to expand upon what she meant.

"Lucy," Adrian sighed. "I just saw Lucy cannibalizing somebody. I don't know what got into her, but the person was dead and she was eating him."

"Hank's Lucy?" Raleigh asked. "The one who's a vegan?" Adrian nodded. "Well, we need to warn people. Don't, like, stand up on a chair and announce what you saw, but go up to each person individually. And you and I can talk later. You'll probably need it."

Normally the quiet, passive employee who let the boss handle big things, Adrian didn't feel comfortable doing this, but knew she needed to take action before it happened again. Taking what she felt was the most logical route, she first approached Nathan.

"Hey, so remember earlier when I told you Lucy wasn't acting so normal?"

"Are you *still* on that, Chase?" Nathan asked,

obviously annoyed that she'd talked to him not once but *twice* within the span of a day.

After having seen the gruesome sight in the hallway, Adrian had pretty much had it, so she replied with, "Listen. I know I'm the typical 'zombie nerd' to all you people, but today has felt a bit off, and the fact that I just saw Lucy eating a dead body's corpse in the hallway doesn't really help me feel more comfortable. I know I sound crazy, but that's the thing and we need a plan."

"You're the zombie fanatic, you do it," was all Nathan could reply.

Assuming Nathan had at least kind of believed her and wanted to survive the rest of the day, Adrian went on to tell Hank what was going on. He deserved to know.

"Are you doing okay, Adrian?" Hank asked after seeing the pained look on her face. She thought about how Hank operated: he processed material in only black and white, high stress really set him off, and this is exactly the kind of thing he didn't need dropped on him.

"So, you remember that book I was reading when you came into my office today?" Adrian began. "What the general premise was?"

"The book was about zombies because all the books you read are about zombies, are you testing my memory right now?" Hank replied, slightly offended.

"You know how they ask does life imitate art or does art imitate life?"

"Your point?" Hank asked, wondering if he

was the only person Adrian could randomly walk up to to talk about zombies.

Telling Raleigh that there was a zombie in the hallway had been difficult, but not nearly as hard as it was telling Hank. Adrian couldn't think of anything to connect this to for him, and worried about what this information would do to him in the long run.

But then, there wasn't necessarily any reason for her to admit that Lucy was the person she found, was there? Pushing aside any thought of how any of this could mess him up, Adrian admitted the truth: she had just witnessed an employee who certainly seemed to have become a zombie.

Zombies were real.

This was a new world that they'd have to survive in.

"Thank you, thank you, thank you," Hank gushed, enveloping a very surprised Adrian in a hug. After a moment, he explained, "I was wondering what was wrong with Lucy. I'm assuming it was Lucy you saw. I noticed she was eating non vegan food, but if her ultimate hope was to eat other humans, then I totally get it. I thought she'd just become a bad person who doesn't care about anything." Which, in the strictest sense *was* true, but not in the way that would have destroyed Hank mentally.

Inwardly, Hank was battling his feelings, trying not to let it show that the love of his life totally changing and becoming a killing machine made him already want to throw in the towel, but he'd learned that, in some cases, it's best to keep those things to yourself. And this definitely seemed like one of those cases to him.

Getting the rest of the group was nowhere near as difficult as it had been to explain the situation to Nathan and Hank; Adrian basically walked up, told them what she saw, and asked if they wanted to survive. It didn't come as a shock that Nick, Lover of Chaos, immediately joined them, seeming excited about what they were about to encounter.

"That means we need Denise, though," he insisted, noticing that she wasn't yet a part of the group. Nick and Denise had somehow become office besties after Nick noticed she was reading a book he enjoyed. The two of them had bonded very quickly, and if not for the fact that Nick was married, would likely have been dating. As it was, they flirted with each other both kind and mean spirited, as friends of opposite genders have been known to do. It wasn't a huge secret that Denise actually thought Nick was attractive, but she knew he was married and was just trying to amuse herself at work.

Adrian had already expended more energy than she had in her getting just *this* small group (being an introvert made her sleeping condition considerably worse), so she told Nick that if he wanted Denise to join, he could talk to her about it.

She watched as he slowly inched toward Denise and put his arm around her shoulder.

"Interesting seeing you here," he said, a classic line he used when talking to her.

"If I talk, are you gonna—excuse me *going*

to—correct my grammar? Or tell me I'm being too wordy?" Denise replied, giving him trouble for his job.

"No, Hank would do that," Nick replied as if it were the most obvious thing in the world. "However, if you submitted something to me in writing and the punctuation was off, then you'd be in trouble, little miss." Denise shoved him jokingly and asked what he wanted.

"Did Adrian tell you what she saw in the hallway?" Nick wondered. "The thing that happened to Lucy?"

Denise replied that, yes, she had been informed of this fact, but didn't feel that a large group of people would be good in this situation. She had been asking around, trying to form a small group of her own, but so far, nobody had agreed to join.

"I mean, the group Adrian has isn't *that* huge," Nick argued once Denise had told him about everybody who had turned her offer down. "And you know I couldn't go on without my office girl." Plus, Nick was all too aware of what kind of person Denise was; she'd venture into the hallway, sure that nobody was going to attack her, and become too cocky, to the point that the first zombie she encountered would immediately be upon her, and probably end up killing her instead of turning her. In truth, she was aware of this fact as well, but figured it would be less painful than trying to survive.

"I mean, I guess if I'm *that* important to you," she finally agreed, not realizing her absence would impact anybody.

"Thank you," Nick sighed. It was bad enough that Hank had lost Lucy; he couldn't even imagine his life without Denise, arguably his best friend.

Nick and Denise returned to the group to find out who else had joined. They had Trevor, who was always down for a good time. Having Trevor might—*might*—help to keep them sane.

Adrian felt both relief and tension when she looked around and realized there were some people who believed her. It was nice having her friend, Hank, and the man in charge at all times, Nathan, but by looking at the two of the men's faces, they had no idea what to do, and were in a state of panic. Still, there was a difference between being the only one who had seen what she had seen, and having a group of people believe what you had seen.

Standing around her was an interesting collection of people ranging all the way from the head nighttime anchor to the woman who covered everything they did about sports. The only issue there was the immediate tension, as Hank did not enjoy being in the company of the person who had absolutely no trouble getting the position he had always dreamed of having. She'd never thought about this before, but the woman who did the reports was also obsessed with fitness. Made sense that she would have gotten that job.

Fortunately or unfortunately, the company therapist was there. While she would be helpful if anybody needed to talk through his or her feelings, she *did* have a tendency to have a holier-than-thou attitude when helping people talk through his or her feelings.

Karl was a familiar face to everyone, making him a nice addition to the group: no matter what, Karl Aster was going to be letting them know what was going on later that night.

Not surprisingly, they had Linda, who was probably just happy to be involved in a large group project, as she primarily worked alone at the end of the reporting process.

And Nancy: the beautiful woman who had bright red hair, shockingly blue eyes, and a body so beautifully proportioned that it was a wonder they'd chosen Karl as the head nighttime anchor.

And a final comfort for Adrian, Nick and Hank, both of whom worked in editing like she did.

Signs were pointing to this not being an epic prank played on this zombie fanatic.

There had been so few people left at the potluck that most of the people in the building either didn't believe what was going on, or were already in trouble. The amount of people who work for the company never much crossed anybody's minds, but seeing how few people they had was a bit disturbing. A glance at the opposite team showed not only a larger crowd of employees, but a group that would likely all become zombies soon. Allen, the man who was in charge of writing the fluff pieces Adrian normally had to fact check, began coughing uncontrollably. Admittedly, it was possible he had swallowed and it had gone down the wrong pipe, or he had a cold, but nobody wanted to wait until the change happened. Adrian thought back to what had happened with Lucy and remembered the thing about her behavior, pulse, and then her leaving the room. A quick glance at Allen's mouth revealed something she wouldn't have expected on any day other than this: teeth that were orange with plaque. Everybody knew everything about everybody, and all knew Allen held great pride in the fact that aside from a time he'd been in the hospital for an extended period, he'd never had a cavity. His normally clean, borderline pearly white teeth today, though, were pretty gross and obviously he hadn't brushed in quite a while.

As this was sinking in for her, Allen stopped coughing but not until a white foam began seeping out of his mouth. It was reminiscent of those cheesy warning videos about rabies, but more likely was a warning that he was infected.

Surprisingly, Allen behaving this way and then getting sick did not get any of the employees who ignored Adrian's warning to join her team. Glancing over at *that* group, she noticed three reporters whose stories she'd fact checked countless times didn't think her facts were exactly right at this time: there was Judy, whose father had introduced her to Monty Python when she was in the fifth grade, resulting in her developing a very weird, primarily British sense of humor. Standing next to her was Tara, who wasn't a writer, but went out into the field and interviewed people for the information she'd then pass on to the writers. She loved her job, but had grown up with parents who didn't let her go out in case she would end up injuring herself. As a result, in her adult life, she ended up spraining her ankle at least twice a year. So she had the zombie walk down, if acting had anything to do with survival. The only other person Adrian recognized by name was a staff writer named Emile, but then she was probably the most memorable person at the company based on appearance: her entire head of hair had never been a normal color. She either had all of her hair dyed some obnoxious color that wasn't natural on people, only segments of it colored, or would have different parts dyed different colors.

The group of nonbelievers was surprisingly large, but none of Adrian's side picked up on any obvious proof that any of them were infected. She forced herself to accept the fact that nobody else was going to join them, and told her team that it was time to move to a different area.

All of a sudden, Hank blurted, "This seems fantastic." For a moment, Adrian assumed that was just Hank unable to control what came out of his mouth, until he went on, "Well face it: you're the one who knows all of the ways to kill zombies, and you're the one who caught it, so obviously you're going to be a great leader."

"You're kidding, right?" Adrian replied. "You think I'm going to be any use in an *actual* zombie takeover? I mean, I'll do whatever I can to help, but we never know what tomorrow will bring. For all we know, we'll be the only survivors. We may just have to never leave this building." She paused, then went on, "That being said, I think we should get out of here and go to my office. We don't know if this disease is airborne or how it even began, but Lucy and whoever that guy was don't come into my office. Everybody use the buddy system: pick one member of our team and keep an eye on each other." Adrian was paired with Hank, Nick took Denise, and those who worked in close proximity to one another also paired up.

Just as they were about to leave the room, Allen passed out. Adrian had a strong suspicion that this was a clear step on the road to becoming a zombie, and urged her team to get out of the room *now*. She told them that they needed to stay as quiet as possible so Lucy and any other turned employees wouldn't be able to hear them. She made a note to take a different route than she'd taken earlier, and they left the room.

On their trip to her office, something occurred to her: without realizing it, she had become these people's hope in a doomed world. She, the quiet one with her nose always buried in a book, was now the leader, helping acquaintances deal with the new world order. She realized that not only had she told them what to do now, but in her head she was planning what she was going to tell them to do once they were secure in her office.

The trip this time went smoother than the one Adrian had gone on earlier in the day. They did not encounter any corpses or infected beings, and Adrian gave them their next instruction. "Call your loved ones. Let them know we're in trouble here and that they should not leave their homes. If they are out, they should go back home. Home is the safest place for them, I don't care if they want to come see you. We'll be locking the building anyway. We only know of two infected employees here and as long as we can keep them at bay, we should be alright. In fact, we aren't even leaving my office."

"But Adrian," Denise said, "isn't 'phone lines going down' one of the first things when zombies happen? Won't we not be able to contact anyone?"

"I was on the phone not an hour ago. I think that since it's so early in the course of events, that sort of thing won't happen for a while. And those are just stories. This is real life. Everything in them could be wrong. And anyway, the infection is different here: the time between whatever happens and when they turn into zombies takes just minutes. And I don't think Lucy was even dead. Just sick and a bit postal. Now she is very postal."

"I have various plugs, if anybody's phone is low on power," Hank announced to the room. Ever the helper, nobody was shocked that he was prepared to help everyone.

Adrian watched as everybody pulled out his or her phone and dialed people to inform them of what was happening. She decided it was a good idea to call Charlie and let him know that her wariness was confirmed by what she saw in the hall. Her husband was everything to her: they had more or less been together since the last few weeks of their senior year of high school. Any time they weren't together, they were thinking about each other.

"I love you," she said when he answered.

"I love you too," he said brightly, clearly in the dark as to what was happening.

"Where are you right now? Are you at home or are you out somewhere?"

"I was just headed to get the cake for tonight," he replied. "I'm heading to the car and—"

"No," she interrupted. "No. Oh God, please tell me you haven't left the house yet."

"Um, no, I'm in the kitchen," Charlie told her. "Why? What's going on?"

"Get in the basement. Right now. Grab some food and water, forget the cake and any other places you were going to go today. Stay there, cover and lock all the doors and windows."

"I know I always say I love it when you get demanding, but that's mostly a bedroom thing. What's going on? This is kind of extreme."

"As is the situation," she said. "Remember how we didn't really end our conversation earlier? That was because I found one of my coworkers chewing on a dead body covered in blood. By which I mean the body and the coworker were covered in blood. Misplaced modifier. Sorry. Charlie, something is happening and it reminds me very much of all of those books we read. Don't go to work, don't go to the car, don't leave the house. Stay. You'll be safer from whatever is going on, at least until we can figure out why and how all of this is happening. At least two of the people here are infected and we're all in a lot of danger. I have a group with me that agreed we need to stay together and are not infected. We're not leaving my office, just trying to lay low. You should do the same. You *have to* do the same."

It took Charlie a moment to believe his wife wasn't just messing around with him, but the desperation in her voice couldn't be faked. And she knew apocalypse. She wasn't just saying this because somebody had gotten a cut or something like that. There was no doubt in his mind that Adrian had encountered one of her coworkers as a zombie. "When will you be home?" he wondered.

"I don't know if I'll ever be home. If I get infected, they'll have to kill me, and I run the risk even worse if I leave the building. But let's agree to contact each other every hour so we know we're alright."

"So I'll talk to you again at one?"

"Hopefully," she said, her voice cracking. "Bye." And she hung up, aware that if she stayed on the phone with him any longer she would burst into tears. Her body shook with the knowledge that she might never see him again. Without any questioning, Hank enveloped her in a hug.

54

Ch. 6
Under Fire

Since a few people were still on the phone when she hung up, Adrian started thinking about what they were going to have to do: figuring out the trick to exterminating this version of the living dead seemed most important.

She thought about the things that were easily accessible in her office: various office and make up supplies, all of the furniture the company provided, and a few things she thought were necessary, such as her phone, her laptop, and some photos of herself and Charlie. If and how these were going to help them, she had no idea. How she and the others could bring themselves to get rid of the people they'd been working with for the past couple of years was even further beyond her comprehension. Nathan had hand picked these employees and they had worked together in close corners for many years. Things were going to get very difficult, very soon.

Looking around the room at the people who had gathered, something occurred to her: she was putting not only herself into quite a situation, but the others as well. Firstly, if whatever had happened to Lucy was a freak incident and nobody else was infected or capable of becoming infected, she'd made a big show out of nothing. Next to that, it occurred to her that she didn't know any of these people in any real sense: they worked together, sure, but how well did any of them *know* each other?

While she knew Hank fine, she and her boss only ever spoke when it was work related, and she barely knew any of those who reported the news or wrote for the paper. She realized, as they all made his or her phone call or calls, that she had no idea who they might be contacting.

It worried her.

Any one of these people could be on the phone to someone who could either come and attack them, or take Adrian away and lock her up in an asylum some place. What she had told everyone felt insane even to herself, who had seen what was happening. And given Raleigh's being a certified therapist and undoubtedly having inside contacts to people who dealt with those who had gone insane, was there anything stopping her from calling one or several of these folks? Add to all of that the fact that it seemed there was no way this many people were willing to believe her story and work together to survive, and Adrian began to stress about it all.

It felt like it took a long time, but after a few minutes, everybody had ended their calls. The discordant thoughts were still clouding Adrian's head, but finally Nancy ended the phone call she was on and said, "So *I'm* engaged now..."

Everybody in the room thought back, remembering Nancy had made it known that she was going to be proposing to Natalie, her girlfriend of five years. They'd been living together for four of those five years, and sincerely seemed like a fantastic couple: any time they had any type of argument, they just took a few hours to let everything settle, then would get back together and talk about it without as much negative energy towards each other. This worked, because living in Springfield didn't give them as much of a dating pool. Although her coworkers didn't know when she was planning on popping the question, the first day of a zombie event seemed about the best choice; it makes the day a little less horrible, and gives a reason to really push to survive.

Adrian laughed.

"Is it fair to assume this isn't exactly how you thought you'd be proposing?" she asked. She felt obligated to open a conversation, in case it needed to happen, as this was unusual in a plethora of ways. While everybody at the company had said they were fine with Nancy's openness about her lifestyle, tensions were pretty high, and times like these were usually when people showed their true colors.

"I wasn't going to do anything as cheesy as your husband did," Nancy said, referencing the time Charlie planned a company party to propose to her. "Actually, I'm sure Nick would love what I had planned: it's always kind of been a thing that when I need to give my significant other one of those bad 'we need to talk' conversations, I do so over a fancy dinner I made. She'd probably end up thinking I was going to tell her something we needed to change, which to be fair I am, but this is a positive change. At some point during the meal, I was going to just take the ring out and ask her to marry me."

"Awesome," Nick said, nodding.

"It would have been so great." As it was, she had called Natalie, asked how she was feeling, then told her to pick up and open the box next to the kitchen sink. Not the proposal she had planned, but *a* proposal, and definitely memorable.

Assuming this subject was finished, Trevor said the thing on everybody's mind. "What now, boss?"

It took Adrian a moment to realize he was speaking to her, as she wasn't used to being the boss and naturally had assumed he'd been talking to Nathan. It felt incredibly weird being their only way to stay safe, and she worried what would happen if any of them did get in trouble through becoming infected by the original source, the infection being airborne, or just being eaten alive by somebody who already had the disease. But for some odd reason, the fact that the most vacuous person in the room wanted to move forward was enough for the rest of them. Everybody loved Trevor, but there was a reason he worked for IT instead of the actual paper.

"Oh, me," Adrian realized after a moment. How she had dreamed of this day: the day the zombies came and everybody looked to her, because of course she'd know what to do, right?

In the fantasies, though, she always pulled out a firearm that she had hidden under her desk, which had never actually been the case: the company did random checks of the offices and such a thing would have gotten discovered and had her in a lot of trouble. And those were all just stupid fantasies. She had neither a firearm, nor an emergency zombie preparedness kit underneath her desk. And she was pretty sure that all of those web pages she had saved about surviving this apocalypse wouldn't actually be helpful. If the internet even still worked.

"Look," she finally said, sitting on her desk, "this is something out of my pay grade. You wouldn't ask Nathan what to do if you had a headache, you wouldn't consult Hank if you were being harassed by a coworker, um... you wouldn't ask Raleigh to report the nightly newscast. No offense. And while I might read about this, I don't know what to do."

"Help us, Adrian Chase," Hank said, getting down on his knees. "You're our only hope."

"While I appreciate the reference, I think we need to work together," Adrian replied. "Please don't put it all on me."

"Fair enough," Hank agreed, standing up. "What book or movie do you think our situation relates to most?" Adrian thought for a moment (there were so many examples to file through) and decided, "Right now, since it's so unreal that this is actually happening, it feels more comical than anything else. It's been so weird up until now: I'm the only one who's seen one of them, and we have a really weird group here. That being said, we know it's not *Warm Bodies*, because that's from the zombie's POV, but it's kind of a combination of *Night of the Living Trekkies* and *Shaun of the Dead*. Sorry, guys."

"How did *they* work out the issues?" Nathan asked, the question on everyone's mind.

"That's why I apologized," Adrian answered. "They really didn't. I mean, in *Shaun* they figured out how to live harmoniously when his best friend turned, but in the other one, they just left the scene and nobody really knows what happened afterward. It seemed to work for them, but it was after an exhausting day of avoiding the zombies, which I'm not looking forward to. But I'm rarely happy with any ending, so don't listen to me about that. That being said, I don't want any of us leaving this room, and I don't think befriending the zombies will work. Honestly, we have to figure out how to get rid of them, and how this infection happened. Not to mention the fact that there could be any number of them out there. The possible sheer mass of infecteds (infectoids?) is... I don't want to think about it. I guess we should start with the how, so we can try to keep it from each other?"

"Staying put *definitely* seemed like a good plan to me," Hank piped in, "although the whole 'locking the building up' thing didn't sound like a bad idea either."

"That can only be done from the main floor," Nathan said in the same emotionless tone they'd all come to know of him at staff meetings. "Somebody is going to have to go down there."

"I'll go," Adrian said flatly. "I have to run to the bathroom anyway. Does anybody else have to go? I don't know how long it'll be until we'll be able to safely leave this room. Probably not for a while."

All of the girls in the room agreed to join, as they all felt they should take the opportunity while it still presented itself. At the last minute, Karl also joined, assuming they'd be learning something that he could report back on.

Adrian reminded them to be silent in the hallway and they headed out, unaware of whether or not they'd get back.

They were hit by a god-awful stench the moment they opened the doors. Nothing even Hollywood could produce. To say it smelled like a mixture of raw sewage paired with a stack of dead fish that had not been properly refrigerated did not do it justice. In their minds they knew that without locking the building up, the source of the stench would only get worse as the amount of casualties grew, but all the same, nobody wanted anything to do with this much needed journey. Each member of the team covered their nose and mouth with whatever type of shirt they were wearing (Denise suddenly found herself genuinely regretting the semi transparent top she'd chosen to wear this particular day) and trooped to the stairwell leading to the lobby.

Without even consciously doing it, Adrian's brain started working out the most important things they'd need to deal with absolutely first: Hank had brain damage that required he take medication twice a day to lessen his epilepsy and chances of seizures, there was obviously *some* common element between everyone who had turned so far, it was possible to identify some weakness aside from going up to a zombie and chopping off its head that brought it down for good, the group was eventually going to need to eat, and everybody in that room had people that they loved and had contacted. She couldn't imagine giving up ever seeing Charlie again, and at least one of the others had just gotten engaged. Over a cell phone call.

Ch. 7
Absence of Malice

"Nancy," Adrian whispered, just loud enough that Nancy would hear. She sped up so that she was directly next to Adrian, then nodded for her to go on. Adrian lowered her voice considerably. "You just asked Natalie to marry you." The rest of the point Adrian was trying to make would be difficult; she couldn't ask if Nancy had a plan about getting them out, but also couldn't just bring up how they were kind of in a hopeless situation.

"I know the chances of us getting out of here are next to none, but I had to do it," Nancy replied, understanding what Adrian was getting at. "I was on the phone to her anyway. I wasn't going to *not* ask her, knowing we may never talk again. Plus, I figured it would be nice for her to have something nice to think about during her last hours alive. And for me. I'm really glad I did it." Adrian gave her a thumbs up, and they continued down the hall in complete silence.

A few minutes later, the whole "being quiet so the zombies won't be able to find us" theory was completely debunked. They saw a zombie (the exact person Adrian had witnessed Lucy eating) lurking around the corner, poised ready to pounce, clearly aware that there was a group of living humans around.

Like most zombies Adrian knew from literature, this one moved clumsily and did not seem the most intelligent being on earth, so the team picked up their pace and entered the first room with a door that locked. A women's bathroom. The men's bathroom was a few feet further away, but this restroom had the extra advantage of being one room with a door that securely locked. Whoever had set up the building did so such that the women's bathroom was a single room that locked: everyone joked that the thought behind this was that girls seemed to care more if people occupied the same general space as them when they used the bathroom, but really it was just that the building didn't have enough space to have two bathrooms with stalls that close together. Even though the door was securely closed and locked, the zombie clawed at the glass, picking up the scent of living humans. The monster didn't think to try the door handle.

Trying to ignore the clawing on the wooden door that was only about an inch thick, Adrian considered what she knew about zombies and what she knew about death. A Simon Pegg fan, *Burke and Hare* was one of her favorite films, and she'd learned a fair bit about body decay from it. Of course she was passively aware that there were different stages of death, the first being rigor mortis, but the film had further educated her about the decay process. Logically, if the first step after death was rigor mortis, it made sense that zombies moved so awkwardly: their limbs were stiff, yet they had the reptilian urge to continue living, which they did by consuming living humans. And living humans weren't so different from them in that way, given the fact that they would oftentimes become paralyzed with fear, as everyone in the bathroom was currently noticing.

Thinking about the zombie right outside the door, however, it didn't seem that it was in that stage. Perhaps it was because zombie-Lucy had done so much damage to the body, but the zombie trying to get in seemed to have passed that step right on to decay, as it had almost no hair, blood that had already dried to a black substance, and on top of missing large chunks that couldn't have been only Lucy's doing, it was completely skeletal. Although it still had skin, the skin was completely pressed up against its ribs, limbs, and neck. Adrian wasn't even sure how the neck was still supporting the head.

Convinced they weren't going to be able to use the rest room in private, Linda (who had already had three cups of coffee) turned on the sink and shrugged stating, "We're all friends here, right?" and went ahead and used the bathroom.

"It's not awkward that I'm here, right?" Karl said after a moment. "Like, you're not all going to feel weird just because I'm the only guy here."

"This is the beginning of a zombie apocalypse," Nancy said, her voice flat. "I don't think 'awkward' is a considerable adjective these days." Agreeing that this was a good plan, everybody took turns taking care of his or her business.

Once that had been finished and they'd all washed their hands and used the hand dryers, the room was strangely quiet.

"Wasn't there just a zombie out there?" Karl asked, putting together the fact that the sound that was missing was that of scratching on the door.

"I guess they don't understand... *doors*?" Adrian said, with less certainty in her voice than she liked. She opened the door a crack and saw the hall had no members of the undead. "Let's go. We have to get to the lobby now, without any more of them finding us." The only question now was why had the zombie given up on them? *Was* it as simple as not knowing how a doorknob worked? Or, were zombies just that juvenile, that the thought of being sanitary and washing one's hands made them stagger away?

They made no contact with zombies on their trek to the lobby, but they also did not see Karen. She must have been getting some food or making a bathroom trip, as no one was at the front desk when they got there. Or, a more likely option, she was infected and out hunting for human flesh. But nobody wanted to entertain that idea.

"Who knows the code?" Denise whispered, barely audible, when they reached the keypad. Being an intern who the boss had entrusted with the code,

Nancy pushed to the front, claiming that she knew it but didn't think anybody else was allowed to know. "You're kidding, right?" Adrian said. "We're dealing with a new world order here and you're worried that Nathan would get mad if somebody else knew how to lock and unlock the doors?"

"Good point," she agreed after a second. "It's 4221. Whoever picked the code was on this weird hipster diet and obsessed with avocados. 4221 is apparently the PLU number for them. Super creative, I know." Adrian punched the code into the keypad on the desk, resulting in a loud clang noise that let them know that it worked. Everybody was beyond grateful that the front of the building was not made of glass and the only way to see if there were infected people trying to get in would be to look at the windowed doors. They of course had absolutely no doubt that there were probably hundreds standing right out of view, but they decided not to think about that.

Adrian took a quick glance to see if there were zombies outside. Sure enough, it wasn't confined to News Sun. Those outside already seemed to have large chunks missing, joints hanging on by a string, and hair falling off of their head as they staggered forward, but she couldn't tell if they'd been infected through a bite. She also made a note in her head of the amount of zombies that were outside; she'd assumed Lucy was the only zombie to start with inside the building, but there must have been a really common thing that got these people in this state—aside from living in Springfield.

"Is everybody ready to go back?" Adrian asked, hoping the others felt better than she did. After seeing all of them, her mind was filled with images of being attacked by the one that had been in front, reaching out to the glass as if there wasn't a barrier between them and the living: she could fully picture it lunging forward with enough energy to break the glass and devour everybody in her group, then taking a huge bite out of her midsection much like the situation Adrian had seen Lucy in earlier this morning.

"I have a thought," Linda said. Everyone waited as she went on, "In classical zombie lore, doesn't the power get cut somehow every time? These doors are closed by electronics."

"Good point," Adrian agreed. Though the building was fairly old, they had installed new electronic locks a few years back to ensure a little more safety at night. The town had enough teenagers and young adults that there had been break ins, resulting only in vandalism, but then, that was never fun for them. She rushed over to the doors, trying to block out the clear sight she had of the zombies, and took a closer look at just the doors. Upon this inspection, she found a separate set of locks: simple ones that turned and could be opened with a key from the outside. Easy for a kid to unlock with a tool when nobody was looking. She made use of these as well, feeling slightly more secure. Obviously in the case that the power did suddenly go out, these would do nothing to stop the zombies from entering the building, but technically in the current time, the doors wouldn't have opened without an employee ID anyway. She laughed to herself, remembering the joke about going to a country club in the case of a zombie apocalypse since no one without a membership could get in. It was considerably funnier before she herself was living through such an apocalypse, but it cheered her up enough to feel ready to get back to her office.

"Okay," Adrian said with a heavy sigh once she was back, "*now* are we ready?" She looked directly at Linda as she said this, then was answered with various nods, shrugs, and groans. Regardless of the lack of consent, they got out from behind the desk and trudged towards the stairs.

There was absolutely no visibility between the stairwell door and the hallway, so nobody had any idea of what was awaiting on the other side. As they approached the door with trepidation, Adrian's shrill ringtone—which was that of an old rotary phone—went off on loud volume, shocking everyone. She snapped it open immediately so it would stop ringing, and answered to find it was the hourly check-up.

"Shit," she said, "I totally forgot. I brought a group out to lock up the building in hopes to keep everyone out." It occurred to her that they still didn't know for certain if the zombies knew how to open doors, and they were currently standing in between two sets of them. If they just stayed where they were, they'd be safe, and there wasn't really any reason for the others to think they hadn't just been abandoned. But she thought of Hank, and how he wouldn't be able to digest that Adrian had abandoned everyone, and she pushed the door open just a fraction of an inch. Surprisingly, there was no evil waiting for them on the other side. She motioned for everyone to follow and held a conversation with Charlie as they made their way back to the room, not once running into the enemy.

"So how are you feeling?" was the first thing Charlie wanted to know.

"Like this isn't a joke," she muttered.

"What was that, hon?" he asked. Adrian sighed.

"I don't know, I guess when I first saw Lucy, I thought—I hoped—that it wasn't true. Someone had put me on a prank show. Somebody knew I love zombies, so they wanted to see just what would happen if it happened to me. How I would respond. But now here we are, what, two hours later, some of my team is already gone, and no celebrity host has showed up to tell me I was fooled. So to answer your question: aside from the awful smell lingering in the hallway, I'm fine. Scared out of my mind and aware that I probably *won't* get out of this, but honestly more worried about you."

"I haven't left the house all day, so unless you have it too, I'm not going to become infected," Charlie assured her. "Assuming the virus is airborne and would be passed through microbes. You just worry about yourself. Has anyone figured anything out yet?"

"They're not very smart," Adrian replied. "They didn't think to try to open the door we were hiding behind, but that's about all I know."

"That's wonderful if it's true," Charlie said, and Adrian could *feel* the relief in his voice. She would have done anything to see him, to know he wasn't infected, to be together once more when she knew they were both alright. Unfortunately, with the building locked down and a much larger population of zombies outside, she knew it wasn't going to happen. She didn't even know how long her phone would last. As they reached her office, they found that the small window on her door had been smeared with blood. Luckily it was on the outside, so nothing violent had occurred *inside* the office. It was probably just another of their futile attempts to get to the living.

"Okay this is super cheesy and I feel bad about saying it, but I miss you," Adrian blurted to her husband once they were back in her office. "I have no way of knowing if I'll ever see you again, or if you'll be dead when I do." She assumed that they'd be stuck in her building for days, weeks or months which would mean that in the case of his death, his body would not be that of the handsome man she'd been with for ten years. It would be bloated, undoubtedly surrounded by flies looking for a nice meal and definitely mostly eaten by a member (or members) of the undead.

"Are you okay?" Charlie asked, interrupting her thoughts. "Adrian if you're crying, there's really not a lot you can do about it. If you're behind a door, you should be alright, right?"

"I love you so much but I *really* have to go,"

she managed to say. "I'll let you know what I find out."

"I love you too and I swear to you that I won't do anything—*anything*—that might even conceivably cause me to become one of them. I am not going to move from this spot and I'm holed up in the basement. I have emergency flashlights and a lot of food with me."

"Genius. Talk to you in an hour?"

"Of course." And the line went dead. Adrian knew he'd be the one hanging up, but didn't like that it had to happen. She stared at her phone as it displayed how long they'd been talking until it went to the main screen, a photo of herself and her husband when they went zip lining.

Ch. 8
State of Play

"Okay," Adrian said, standing in the front of the room, "I don't know about you all, but I think we need to make a plan so we feel a little better. I feel pretty hopeless right now, and I don't want to feel this way."

After receiving a consensus, Adrian erased all of the information written on her white board, trying not to think about the fact that none of that information she had would be pertinent in this new world. She quickly jotted down everything she'd already worked out in her head (adding a note about picking up Nancy's fiancé at the bottom, just as a reminder to herself), and made a color guide: green was 'probably should be considered' and red was 'most important.'

The first thing she wrote in red was 'medicine'. She knew that people who truly needed his or her medication often kept a spare supply on hand, but there was no way of knowing how long they were going to be stuck here.

"Why are you using the white board?" Trevor asked. "I'm just wondering. You've got a computer right there."

"We're dead meat," Adrian said, her voice lacking in tone. "A computer isn't going to help us right now. Even if I did put all of this information on it, it might run out of power."

A while later, the board was filled with words: the top was filled up with the questions of medicine, food, communication with the outside world, what they would do when someone had to use the bathroom, how to kill, and how the infection began. There was a mutual agreement not to worry about anything outside of the room for the time being and they prepared to talk about what they'd do for medicine. Debating what deserved to be on this list and what needed to be in what color had taken a sizable amount of time, so it was just about time for Adrian and Charlie's hourly check up. And this time *she* wanted to be the one making the call.

She opened her phone and dialed his number, terrified she wasn't going to get an answer. She fought back tears as the phone rang and she realized that none of the people in the zombie books she'd read had as close relationships with people as she had with her husband. They'd been together since the end of their senior year in high school.

He answered the phone, immediately stating that he was still alright and wondering what they were doing in the office to keep themselves safe. She explained how they had been working together in planning what to do going forward but they were still no closer to figuring anything out.

"So you're sure you don't have a sudden hunger for human flesh?" Adrian asked. "Nothing's been out of the ordinary on your end?"

"Nothing I noticed," he answered. "I think I'm safe, but if I'm being honest, I *am* hugely curious about what it's like out there."

"No, don't," Adrian immediately said. "I am beyond terrified here at the office where I was unlucky enough to have witnessed some of the transformations and what they do once they're on the other side of humanity."

"I'll stay," he agreed. "I don't need to see that, I'll just watch *Shaun of the Dead* or something." They had a mutual love for zombie literature, though Adrian's passion for it definitely overpowered his. Since he hadn't been through any of the attacks that Adrian had, he was actually excited about the fact that this was happening, but that could all change with just a glance outside.

"As much as I'd like to talk to you forever, I don't know how long my phone will work if I stay on it for too long. We'll keep in contact through the day but I'll call you if anything important happens in terms of figuring *anything* out."

"Good luck." Each phone call they had became slightly easier: a simple "are you undead? No? Okay, see you soon" was what it had essentially become, and they weren't arguing about whether or not what Adrian was saying was true. She had little doubt that they'd be talking to each other again. She hung up and returned to her coworkers.

"Medicine," she said with a deep breath. "What sort of issues do we have here?"

"My asthma's been fairly under control as of late," Trevor said. "I don't usually have asthma attacks anymore, and I have enough in my inhaler to last for a while."

"So you're taken care of. Who else (aside from Hank) has medical problems?"

"I'm not officially on any type of medication for my emotional issues," Karl told them. He held his hand in the "live long and prosper" position from *Star Trek*. "I solemnly swear I'll do everything I can to not go off on you guys."

"Much obliged," Adrian muttered, knowing it was completely out of his control. "Anyone else have anything we should know about?"

"Well I wasn't done," Karl interrupted. "I have an allergy and a migraine condition. They kind of work together, but in short, I can't have blueberries. I'm allergic to them. It's horrible."

"Right, then. So basically Karl is a low key version of Hank in terms of medical issues. You done?" She paused for effect. "Anyone else?" She was met with absolute silence, so they agreed to move on to the next consideration: food.

Everybody had packed enough food for their lunch that day and a few of them had snacks because they tended to get hangry, but nothing that could sustain them for more than a day or two. There was a cafeteria on the first floor which had the typical non perishable foods they served on a regular basis, but that was pretty far away.

"We're going to have to get food," Adrian said. "I've got this fridge here, so we can grab some things that require refrigeration."

"Food," Karl said. "You mean like the substances we have a room full of literally one floor up?" Linda groaned, for she was not a huge fan of his, either.

"You mean the room where Lucy the zombie just ate a bunch of cheeseburgers?" she argued. "I don't think we should go anywhere even in close proximity to that."

Trying to stop a fight that could have easily started, Raleigh intervened. "Can we wait until we know how to kill the zombies before we leave here?"

"Shot to the head," Karl said blankly. "Everybody knows that. I'll definitely come on the trip, by the way."

Adrian suddenly had the exact same overwhelmed feeling that she did constantly when she had to spend endless nights in the hospital, trying to figure out what was wrong with her. At least in those cases, none of the things currently on her white board were issues. Realizing this, she convinced herself that it would be more hopeless if it were one of the times she was stuck there, as she'd have to figure out how to unplug herself from the machines, and hospitals are far larger than the office building in which she worked. All at once, she imagined how she would feel if she were in the hospital right now, leaving her with the feeling of a crushing defeat, although nothing had gone wrong yet.

This feeling only got worse as a strange pounding sound at her door caused her to glance over and see about three of her now undead co-workers trying to get in, scratching at the door with the bloody stumps that were left of their fingers. She knew that for the time being there was nothing they could do. If the zombies knocked the door in, they'd eat everybody in Adrian's office.

She sat on the floor right in front of her desk, as did many of the others. Nobody said anything or made any movement in the hopes that the zombies would assume nobody was around, or just give up trying to claw the door down, as they didn't even have nails.

The awful silence was interrupted as somebody shrieked when a fluorescent light went out above them. Adrian cringed, knowing there were zombies trying to get in directly outside her thin door.

"Yeah I've been meaning to change that," she muttered. The bulb had been on the fritz for a few days. It must have finally given up. "Everybody hush, do you hear that?"

There was no more pounding at the door and there didn't appear to be a shadow of any figures standing right outside, meaning the zombies had moved on.

Ch. 9
Final Edition

"Um guys, I think we figured something out," Adrian said warily. "Remember in the hallways, how we were pretty quiet but that one found us? Then they left when we ran the sink? Maybe it *wasn't* just because they don't like sanitation. And then just now. We weren't being *that* noisy but they figured out where we were, but left when you screamed. New plan: be as loud as you can. It's a good solution. At least for now."

Denise broke the silence, complaining, "Yeah I'm really not going to be wanting to walk down the hall if I have to use the bathroom. There are probably *a lot* more of them by now. Even if we know how to get rid of them."

Adrian bit her lip, realizing how odd it was that this had never been something they mentioned in any of the books or movies she enjoyed.

It sort of made sense; a lot of the stories only

covered the first few hours of the apocalypse, which was always an easy enough time to find a bathroom. It would have been really helpful if they didn't all gloss over that, but of course nobody would have known that to ever be relevant information in the real world. A lot of them switched perspective on and off, and she'd always inferred that the other characters used the bathroom when they weren't the one in the narrative.

She was never going to watch another zombie movie.

If she did get home, she was going to throw away—no shred—no *decimate*—any and all zombie related things she had: the stickers in her car windows, the posters next to the bed she and Charlie shared, even the fan art her friend had done for her.

"So we're on the second floor," Adrian said. "Leaving this room is something we don't want to do for *any reason* excessively. Like, we'll go to get food but get *a lot* so we'll be taken care of for an extended period of time."

"Could we hurry this up? I've made the mistake of trying to drink 64 ounces of water a day, and that on top of coffee...," Nathan interrupted. Adrian's eyes flashed to the trash can she had in her office; a wire mesh thing that had a few used tissues and scraps of paper in it. It barely worked as a trash can, let alone a makeshift toilet.

There was a mostly empty 16 ounce lemonade jug in her fridge. She grabbed it and it shoved into Nathan's hands.

"Modesty went out the window with Lucy's

vegan habits," she muttered.

Nathan nodded slightly, but went to the other side of the room to do his business. "Do we have any germaphobes here?" Adrian asked the room in general in order to distract everyone from the tinny sound of urine hitting glass. She was greeted with a chorus of 'nos' and asked, "So is everyone comfortable with that solution? Given our situation?"

"Great thinking, Chase," Nathan said, returning to the group, holding the jug, which only had a small bit of urine in it, but Adrain found rather gross. It reminded her of those times she'd had to give urine samples in the hospital; there was hardly anything in it, but it was full enough. She never thought it was fair that men had a much easier time filling those stupid containers.

Once Nathan had returned from the window, Hank asked, "Can I borrow that now?" Nathan shrugged and handed it over, thinking about how weird it is that this would be how life is lived. This was now the protocol when somebody had to use the bathroom.

"Um, actually I'm going to go out into the hallway," Hank said, pointing vaguely to the door.

"I think if we can handle our boss peeing in a jar right in front of us, it's socially acceptable for you to do it as well," Adrian let him know.

"That's not why I'm going out there," he answered morosely, setting the jar down. "They can have me. I surrender."

Fuck, Adrian realized, processing that the

woman Hank had been in love with for the past five years had just turned into Patient Zero. And he'd seen every step of her transformation earlier in the day. He'd devoted much of his career trying to get higher up so they would be working in the same area, a task he could realistically never accomplish given his brain damage.

"Hank. Stop." She blocked the door so he wouldn't be able to exit the room, thinking she could make him see this realistically. "Stop it. *We* can still survive."

"Okay, point one: I already look like a zombie." He gestured angrily at his face. "If anyone outside of us sees me, they'll shoot me on sight. That is one of the first things I felt like when I got this injury."

He was speaking in understandable, thought out sentences. Clearly he meant business.

"Point two: now there's *absolutely* nothing left for me. Not only did Lucy turn, I didn't have anyone else beside her. And you *know* Jennifer just told me she's getting married. Get out of the way." She knew there was no changing his mind, that he no longer felt there was a reason to live, so she stepped aside and allowed him to exit.

There was a deafening silence in the room for a few minutes as a sense of rubatosis overtook all of them, each and every person's heartbeat clearly audible in his or her own head, until Adrian glanced out the window to discover there were about five of the undead crouching in a circle, tearing the meat off of something that she desperately pretended wasn't

Hank's corpse.

Once they'd gotten all that they wanted and shambled down the hall, Adrian opened the door to see what remained of the body. What had just hours ago been a spry man with life in his eyes looking toward the future was now a corpse with limbs missing, large chunks torn out of his body, and blood stained in an uncomfortable amount of places. The sight was horrific, far worse than anything else they'd encountered that day. Adrian had really liked him; she was rooting for him to hook up with Lucy the entire time. He was just a little guy, he didn't deserve what just happened.

"We need a way to kill these fuckers," she announced, starting to pace the room. The adrenaline pumping through her body was making it difficult for her to keep still. "Hank is dead. And he's not coming back: not even as one of them. He's gone forever."

Once she thought about that, Adrian glanced at the Bible Verse A Day calendar that was sitting on her desk and wondered: where did the soul go if a person became a zombie? And, more importantly, if a severely depressed individual gave in to the zombies, where did his soul go?

The book of Matthew had a passage, she knew, about those who are considered last receiving eternal life in Heaven if they had been believers. She knew that Hank suffered for much of his life, but didn't think he had ever outwardly denied God's existence. Although his functionality was not what it had been before his brain injury, he still had a steady job, people who loved him, and was an inspiration to many. Suddenly, the floodgates opened: Hank was not just an unprofessional and constantly upset employee to Adrian, he was a friend. The two of them had worked together for such a long time and had their in-jokes and office gossip they would discuss on a regular basis. If not for the fact that she so wanted to see her husband again, she wasn't sure she wouldn't have just done exactly what Hank did. Her friendship with Hank was common knowledge around the office, so nobody was shocked by her sudden reaction.

Hank had been a wonderful man. His life, however, hadn't been that great.

"It will be alright," Trevor said, approaching Adrian who was now a heap on the floor. He wrapped his arms around her, hoping the warmth would remind her that they were all okay and completely on her side and continued, "This definitely sucks, and we'll be losing many more people in the coming days." She couldn't gather herself; Hank had been a big part of what had kept her going so far. "We're all here together and we'll support each other. We won't let anything like this happen again."

"He's right," Raleigh said, kneeling down on her other side. "You were definitely right to let him do that, but we need to think about how the rest of us are going to survive. If we get hung up on anybody we lost, we'll lose the ability to keep the surviving members safe." Raleigh obviously knew a lot more about where Hank's thoughts had been leading, but Adrian still felt bad about just letting him give up. She should have tried harder to stop him. She knew why he gave up and she fully supported it, she just hadn't considered what it would do to her personally. She couldn't believe that just yesterday he had been joking with her about the fact that political comics went over most politicians' heads. And seeing the remains: it was all far more graphic than anything she'd seen in movies. And the fact that she both knew *and* liked the guy just added to the horror.

"I have a thought," Linda said, also approaching her. "Why don't you give me your phone and I'll get your husband on the line for you? He knows you better than we do; he's probably going to be more helpful than any of us."

There was something about the fact that she's spoken to this woman all of three times in four years, but how she suddenly was so invested in keeping Adrian safe that gave Adrian strength. She lifted a shaking hand and reached into her pocket for her phone.

Ch. 10
True Crime

One of the great things about Charlie was that he always seemed to know ahead of time when something was wrong.

"What's going on now?" he asked by way of answering the phone.

"Hi, is this Adrian's husband?" Linda asked politely.

"Yes, how's she doing?" he wondered.

"Not great. She's not infected or anything, but she... she just really needs to talk to you." She handed the phone to Adrian who still could not hold it together.

"Adrian," Charlie said, "Adrian, babe, what's going on? Talk to me, honey." She loved pet names, and needed coaxing.

She was at a loss for words. She'd seen it happen, witnessed it happening, but she couldn't bring herself to say it.

"It's... Hank," she managed.

"He turned?" Charlie assumed.

This idea brought on a fresh wave of tears, now flowing more freely than they had before as she thought again about that mangled corpse just outside of her door. Her mind was telling her that it almost would have been better if he'd turned; that way he'd no longer have any place in society and his death would be necessary to keep everyone safe. As it was, she knew some unlucky janitor was going to discover what was left of him and have to either call in the big guns or up and carry away and dispose of whatever was left of the body and clean up the giant blood stains in the rug.

Charlie realized very quickly what had happened. Although he did not know how and could tell Adrian did not want to discuss it with anyone, he knew he had to help.

"What can I do to make it better?"

Adrian didn't think it was possible, but Linda had been right about Charlie's ability to help. He never liked bringing this up, but felt this was one of those times that he didn't have much of a choice.

"Close your eyes."

Adrian did as she was told.

"Halloween week, senior year," Charlie said with a cringe. It was the day he had asked Adrian on a date. He was dressed as an expendable ensign, she was dressed as Bob Woodward. The two of them were both awkward high schoolers, but Charlie had it a little bit worse, as he was a trekkie, and not quiet about the fact. They were both in American Sign

Language 2, after taking American Sign Language classes together for two years. It's a very expressive language, and Adrian picked up on the fact that Charlie wasn't feeling super well, based on his facial expressions and body language. She'd signed "Are you okay?" to him, to which he replied "Ask after class." He asked her what she was going as for Halloween to get the conversation rolling, then asked (very nervously) if she'd consider spending time together that night, then on Friday, going to the Halloween dance as his date. He'd put it off until two days before the event, truly thinking she would say no, and didn't know what to do with himself when she said yes.

"High School Charlie had no idea of the life he had to look forward to," Adrian laughed, starting to feel better. "He was super cute, though. High School Adrian kind of had always had a crush on him."

"*She* could have asked *him* out," he said, not for the first time.

"I know," she laughed. "Anyway, babe, I kind of need to tell my team what we're going to do next," she went on, pulling herself together a little bit more. She was still the leader. "You're sure you're not infected?"

"I haven't left my space in the basement," he assured her. "And I'm in the corner furthest away from the door, which is closed. I feel fine and I haven't seen any of the things you've seen."

Adrian felt solace knowing her husband had not only taken her at her word, but was doing everything he could to keep himself safe.

Again, Adrian and Charlie were forced to end their conversation far sooner than they would have liked because they wanted to save the phone batteries and there was more going on than just the two of them. Adrian's gut knew she really should be upset, but tried to only focus on how cute and awkward her husband had been the first time he'd asked her out.

Trying to think about nothing but that adorable memory, Adrian got up on her desk, planning to make an announcement to the room.

"Okay, everybody," she said, "things are getting worse. I think it's only a matter of time before more of us go through something like Hank just did. I, for one, would probably do the same thing if I didn't still have Charlie waiting at home. That being said, we need a plan. We need to avoid what just happened happening again. It doesn't seem that any of us are infected, so we won't be going down the way Lucy and the others will have to eventually."

One of the worst parts was knowing that nobody was coming to save them. It was every man for himself in this world, and who knew what was just beyond those doors? In a world where zombies are a reality, who knew how soon everything else would be a reality? Not to mention the degenerates who would clearly not get the disease because they'd have no problem killing anything that even approached them.

With the awareness that at least two of the building's employees were infected, there were sure to be more. Sure, all the books discussed how a zombie's favorite part is the brain and that the corpse did not become a zombie if the brain was eaten, but who knew how many brains a zombie could devour per day? And considering Lucy, who hadn't had any meat in six years, was out there eating brains, she would either eat less brains and cause more zombies, or there would be a ton of human body parts remaining in the hallway.

Adrian was insanely thankful for this small group of people looking up to her, willing to follow the directions she gave them and help each other stay alive. Sure, it wasn't a huge group, but she had a much better feeling with this bunch of people than she had alone in the hall earlier in the day.

"Those poor families," Adrian said hollowly after a bit of silence. "There was no way of saving any of them. Everyone's doomed."

"Shit," Nick said, the first to understand Adrian's meaning. He glanced into the building's parking lot and saw exactly what he hoped he wouldn't: an empty yellow school bus which had arrived that morning, packed with fourth-grade children, all of whom were now somewhere inside the building. He thought back to his fourth grade years and how excited he and his classmates used to get about going on field trips. The fourth graders visiting today were as aware as any of News Sun's employees about what would come of this exciting field trip. As it stood, the members of whatever classes were visiting not only didn't have school today, but probably would never have to attend another class again.

"You work in editing as well, correct?" Nick said. Adrian nodded, completely unaware of where he was going with this question. "Well just think of this situation as a piece with a bunch of factual inaccuracies. You adjust whatever needs to change and leave in whatever is right, right?"

"What *are* you?" Adrian asked, absolutely baffled that someone as simple as this Nick person could come up with something as profound as that.

"We're all editors," Nick said with a shrug. "You would do fact checks, ensuring absolute accuracy to avoid libel, trimming unnecessary words and correcting inconsistencies. Hank wrote the headlines, ensured fairness and ever so eloquently removed passages that were in poor taste, and then it all got sent to me. I would check punctuation and make sure the pieces conformed to the house style. That was my thing. And no offense to either of you, but I always felt obligated to check on what you guys checked."

Adrian couldn't help but laugh at the idea of what the article about this all would read like, not to mention having to come up with an appropriate headline. She could see it now: Zombiegate. This Just In: A Zombie Story. The Undead Man. It would probably be printed in Times New Roman. She'd have to ask Linda her take on the font later. Who would Nathan have had her call to make sure it wasn't just staged now?

Still, none of it made sense: they were a news company. How did they not notice any clues that a zombie apocalypse was upon them?

"So what's the plan, then?" Nathan wondered, derailing Adrian's train of thought.

"We're going to have to go out and figure out how we start exterminating them," Adrian answered aloofly, beginning to understand that the zombies no longer mattered as humans. She knew it wasn't technically safe in her office, that more and more people were getting infected while they hid out, and they had to put a stop to it. She thought about all the "easy saves" in the zombie books and movies she'd read or seen through the years: the discovery of a weapon someone had kept hidden in his desk, a fully functional gun that had only been used as a decoration, the ability to train a zombie or change it; how she longed for an easy save like that. She'd never fired a gun, but felt a gun would certainly be more handy than the stapler she'd found in her bottom drawer. Being such a small town, no one in Springfield knew much about defending themselves or thought about defense in any extreme way.

"Who has anything on them that can be used as a weapon?" She waited as people rummaged through their purses and bags, pulling out anything they could find that might help. Her desk filled up with cosmetic supplies, coins, a couple of heavy duty wallets, and other assorted junk.

It was better than nothing.

Ch. 11
Good Night and Good Luck

"I don't have it with me, but I keep a radio in the basement," Trevor said as Adrian surveyed everything on her desk. "Might come in handy when your cell phone dies. I don't know."
A life long *Gilligan's Island* fan, Trevor was very interested in communicative technology and liked to know where all of the modern things people use came from. As a person who always bought the cheapest cell phone and cell phone plan he could, he got enjoyment out of knowing other ways to communicate than talking on the phone. Nine times out of ten, he would do video calls over Facebook or Skype, but it did feel to him like the internet and cell towers weren't going to be viable for much longer.
"Tell me more," Adrian said. She knew her phone wasn't going to last forever, and that old fashioned devices could be helpful as a failsafe in certain times. Not that Charlie had an old radio just laying around to use when her phone died, but maybe there was another person in town they could contact.
Trevor launched into a history of radio

communications, what kinds of radios he had at home, what he kept here, and how it might be helpful for all of them in their predicament. Basically, he could send out signals in Morse code to let anyone listening know that they were in trouble, and then what station they would need to go to in order to speak over it.

"So kind of like a weird version of a walkie talkie," Trevor summarized with a shrug. "Any interest?"

"We need to get that right now," Adrian said. "And if we kill a few zombies along the way, great."

Everybody stood around uncomfortably, not wanting to leave the safety of the room. "Okay, how is everybody feeling physically?" Adrian went on when nothing happened. Nobody had any complaints until Nathan's nose started bleeding.

"Oh my gosh, Chase, how dry is this room?" he asked, crimson red dripping down his face.

"My office... it isn't dry," Adrian replied, knowing what this bloody nose had to mean. "Nathan, didn't you say you had an allergic reaction last night? That that's why you were late this morning?" He nodded as he retrieved one of the packages of tissue that somebody had put on Adrian's desk.

"Don't do that. Lay down." If her suspicion was right, next he would pass out (she still couldn't make herself believe the people actually died before coming back), then come back as a zombie.

Nathan obliged, still trying to stop the steady flow of blood coming out of his nose. It wasn't like

Nathan to give in to another person's authority, and Adrian was all too aware that she had to do whatever she could to make this as painless as possible for everybody. She didn't like Nathan as much as she'd liked Hank, but tried to look at the fact that this was happening exactly like it had with Lucy—and right in front of her—as a good thing.

She could use Nathan to figure out how to do away with them.

As she had expected, Nathan was unconscious (dead) a few minutes later, so Adrian announced what was going on.

"Everybody, Nathan is about to turn. We're going to use him to figure out how to get rid of the others."

"How do you know?" Denise asked.

"He got a bloody nose, then passed out, and come to think of it, he wasn't acting like himself today: he was late to work and had seemed to be enjoying the potluck about as much as the rest of us," she answered. "He's following the exact pattern of what happened with the others. So we'll be using him when he's conscious again."

After a few minutes, he was awake, and Adrian saw the same hunger in his eyes she'd seen in Lucy's. In an attempt to stop him from injuring anyone, Nancy chucked one of the wallets at him, only causing him to tilt his head as if challenging one of them to do something worse. Denise walked over and rammed her foot as fiercely as she could into the side of his head, which did nothing but make a moist noise that grossed everybody out.

Suddenly remembering the shitty things Nathan had said to her when she first started working on the paper, Adrian grabbed a handful of coins and threw them at him fiercely. It would hurt a living human, but what effect would it have on the undead?

The coins sunk into whatever his head had become and he sank to the ground. The bad news, however, was that his head then discharged a green vapor that emitted a smell similar to the chemical smells Adrian was all too familiar with from the hospital. No matter which hospital it was, regardless of how long she was there, that smell was always there. She couldn't escape it.

She staggered backward, not wanting to have any type of memory of those visits, and decided not to try anything like that again.

"That actually worked?" Karl said, trying not to accept that Adrian had a good idea. "That's actually kind of awesome. Can I do it next time?"

"Now the question is whether that happened because of how many I threw, or if it was the specific metal in one of the coins. And if we could use one per zombie," Adrian observed. "Maybe just one would have a better effect."

"Try Frisbeeing it next time," Nancy suggested with a shrug.

"Maybe if we could fashion a sling shot, that would work, too," Linda observed. "Are there any rubber bands?"

"I like those ideas," Adrian agreed, thinking of when something like that worked in one of her movies. She rummaged around in her top drawer and pulled out a few rubber bands and pencils, which she gave to Karl. "Make a sling shot while we walk. We ready to go?" Everybody muttered agreements and began to gather the rest of the coins from the table.

"Do we want to leave his body here, assuming he won't reanimate?" Linda asked. Adrian had been preoccupied, realizing that by opening that door, she would be seeing what was left of Hank. She hadn't even thought about how hard it was to kill a zombie for good.

"Drag him into the hallway. If he's still there when we get back, great. If not, that's great too." It was clear that she didn't actually believe any of this, as she was basically using the tone one uses when talking to a small child. She was still thinking about what she might see of Hank.

Karl, Linda and Trevor grabbed various limbs and picked him up, carrying him to the door. He'd been a rotund man, and wasn't a pleasure to carry.

Adrian forced herself to open the door, learning that it *was* possible to feel worse than just knowing she'd let Hank give up. There was nothing left of his body. Everything he'd been had been devoured by someone who used to work for the company.

100

Ch. 12
How to Lose
Friends and Alienate People

The more she thought about it, the weirder it got: she, a well known zombie fanatic was here during the apocalypse, drawing on what she'd seen in entirely fictional movies, trying to figure out the rules.

"Weren't there a lot of people calling in sick these past few days?" Raleigh said. As the company's social worker, it made sense that she would notice this.

Adrian remembered that before any of this nonsense had started, Hank mentioned that Lucy had been out for a few days. Could there be any connection between her absence and this apocalypse? Upon realizing this, Adrian figured that they should begin to look at the news that they had been reporting on in the past few days to see if there might be anything there.

It was getting later in the day at this point, around the time that they would normally start reporting on the major news stories. With everything that had happened and with Nathan gone anyway, nobody had realized this. She hadn't been able to get around to the fact check, anyway. Nathan would have been pissed.

"Good thinking, Raleigh," Adrian agreed. "I think you may be on to something." She pulled out her phone and opened a note taking application she had.

"Nathan was late," Adrian said, typing his name in. "I know that."

"I've got the complete list right here," Raleigh said, pulling out her PDA. She kept track of those who missed multiple days of work on the case that they were "calling in sick" with some mental baggage she needed to meet with them about.

"Let's see... it was Carrie first, then Dan, followed by Jared..." She scrolled for a moment before adding, "And then Lucy. She was the last to call in. Carrie, Dan, and Jared never came back. We assumed they were doing that whole 'ghosting your job' thing."

Once they had the name of everybody who had been absent within the past two weeks, they got to work mapping out each of the employees' relation to one another, assuming there were any.

Somewhere in the midst of trying to figure this puzzle out, Adrian called Charlie again, this time because she realized her family may not know yet.

"I don't see how they couldn't," came Charlie's answer. "I haven't been out all day and there is evidence of it. There's nothing running on television right now besides reruns of bad TV shows, there have been multiple... *things*... scraping at our door, and something smells awful directly outside. I keep having to run upstairs to use the bathroom." Ever since she'd known him, Charlie'd had a nervous bladder. Any time he was overly stressed or anxious about even the littlest thing, he would have to use the bathroom almost every five minutes.

"You realize you're alo... okay, never mind," Adrian said, wondering why he'd bother going upstairs to pee, reasoning that in his mind, they'd be returning to their home once all of this was over. "But our parents. If they don't know, they'll know soon enough," Adrian realized, defeated. "*At least* call them, okay?"

"Will do." Adrian was getting ready to hang up until she heard him continue. "And Adrian? Adrian, don't worry, we are smart people, as are our families. We'll find a way out of this." It meant a lot but it would have meant considerably more if she hadn't grown up with her parents saying similar things about figuring out why she couldn't get good enough rest at night.

"Thanks, Charlie," she said. "Talk to you later." She hung up the phone and they went back to charting out the relations between the employees they thought might be infected so far.

"Can I ask why we're bothering with this instead of figuring out how to stay alive?" interrupted one of the employees Adrian had seen at the picnic earlier and actively decided not to approach.

"Well sure," Adrian replied, not showing that this sudden question had upset her. "I figured that if any of these people had worked in close quarters, we'd be able to tell how it got spread."

"I'm not seeing you as a very good leader right now," the employee (Karl, Adrian remembered) went on. "You're clearly just trying to look like you're doing something important when you really have no idea what's going on."

It was well known around the office that Karl was a difficult person. As a head reporter, he had a fairly large ego, so the fact that Adrian was running everything right now did not sit well with him.

Resisting the intense urge to slam her hand on the table and completely go off on him, Adrian instead took a deep breath and said, "Okay, clearly being cramped up in here is starting to get to us. And last time we were out there, it was just to try and defeat some of them." She herself wasn't doing too well and knew it was only a matter of time before someone had some sort of mental breakdown. "If anybody's siding with Karl, they can help lead the expedition to get us all some food."

"And where will you be?" Denise inquired.

After some consideration, Adrian said, "I need out for a while too, and I think we tend to do better in large groups. So if you're feeling even a little restless, please join. I'm not feeling up to being in charge of this scouting party, is the thing." Her sleep deprivation was really starting to rear its ugly head, given the fact that her brain had been running nonstop since she'd seen Lucy eating a cheeseburger. She was beginning to feel foggy, and (even though she knew it wouldn't help) just wanted to curl up on the floor and go to sleep.

In the end, it ended up being a group with Adrian, Karl, Denise, and Nancy, again leaving four people in the office and Adrian once again forced to consider how quickly their numbers were diminishing. So few of the employees had believed her when she said what was going on and then they'd lost two.

"Get over it, Chase," she whispered to herself, gripping the coins in her hands even tighter. It hardly took any time at all for a group of zombies to sniff them out, causing those still alive to start throwing coins before the undead could start attacking. They quickly discovered that the "shoot for the head" thing was legit but it really worked best if they were nailed directly in the forehead.

Within minutes, there was a stack of (hopefully) actual corpses in the middle of the hallway, which the team carefully stepped over, unsure of what to do next.

106

Ch. 13
The Paper

Trying not to think about how much the smell in the hall reminded her of the hospital, Adrian mentioned something. "We're going to need more coins."

As they continued walking, they passed the coin machine in the vending area. It didn't really get used and had just become a part of the scenery in the hallway.

Trevor walked up to the machine, grabbed it by the sides and pulled, trying to tip it over. Adrian knew he was just taking out his frustration on the machine, but still grabbed him from behind and pulled him away, picturing it tipping over and crushing him to death.

"At least push it *away* from yourself!" she yelled, shoving him at the machine. "But don't even; we need you and honestly Denise is the only one here who even has any chance at fighting that thing."

Denise, the only person present who exercised on a regular basis, laughed at the idea of tipping over a machine that weighed far more than she could lift, plus the fact that there probably weren't many coins in it anyway.

"Call your husband," Trevor mumbled, trying to avoid being embarrassed further by her outrage. Adrian had been looking forward to her next call, and pulled out her cell phone, thinking the call *might* have been past due, but sure he'd answer no matter what.

"It's getting worse," she said upon his answer. "We lost Nathan, too. Should have seen it coming."

"Don't blame yourself," Charlie answered in the voice that'd made her fall in love with him. "It's the first day we've known about this. Of course some things are going to surprise you."

"I want out of this," Adrian complained.

"Well at least you have something to do," Charlie replied. "I've been stuck in my corner all day, just wondering what's going on outside."

In truth, Adrian envied him for not having to have faced this at all, but after those weeks she'd spent stuck in a hospital room not able to go outside for even two minutes for a breath of fresh air, she knew how he must be feeling.

"I understand, but we still don't know how this is spread and I just feel a lot better knowing you're staying there," Adrian said. "Maybe now that we at least know what hurts them, you could go upstairs if you *needed* to, but I still think this is good."

"As awful as this is, there is one good thing that came out of it," Charlie mentioned. Adrian couldn't figure out what he could possibly mean until he went on, "Now we don't have to go to that family picnic."

She chuckled.

Even now, after five years of marriage and a few hours of a zombie apocalypse, he was able to make her laugh. "Anyway, hang in there, we'll figure something out."

"Thanks," she said, feeling marginally better.

"Yeah, just don't think about any of this and maybe sleep or something. I'm just trying to figure out what we need in order to stay healthy."

"Don't worry about me," he answered. "There is nothing else alive in the house (I *did* release Dwight like you told me to) and I haven't even opened a window."

"And how are you feeling?" Adrian managed to ask. She dreaded that he might say that he had a stomach condition or headache at the moment. His answer did nothing to ease that fear.

"I don't know if you're ready to hear my answer to that," he said apologetically. "The news isn't good." It felt as if somebody had just told her she was only expected to live another three days. Adrian couldn't fathom her life without Charlie; he was the love of her life and if anything happened to him, she wouldn't see any reason to continue.

"Just tell me," she said. "I can't feel much worse than I do now." Charlie took a deep breath before giving his answer.

"Remember how I was feeling last night before I went to sleep?" She did remember: he hadn't eaten well at all in the day, actually skipped out on dinner, and had a migraine so bad that he was nearly throwing up (dry heaves, given that he didn't have any food in him). Adrian had forced him to eat something and drink a lot of water, hoping that was all his body needed. She'd forgotten about that until now and wished she hadn't asked. Normally, he would go to urgent care if this were the situation, but he had a suspicion that urgent care probably wouldn't see him, given the situation.

"So you're not doing any better, then?" she assumed. "Do you need me to come home? All the people I have here can fit into two cars, maybe one, and—"

"No Adrian," he interrupted, "stay where you are. The fact that I'm not feeling well is kind of proof nothing's wrong. Honestly I was just planning on vegging out aside from my plans to pick up the cake. If you do end up coming home you can get me, but for now just stay at work and don't get it in your head that the reason I'm not feeling well is because I'm infected. I mean, you know me: I don't ever do anything or go anywhere so there's not much of a chance I got it."

"But your store!" she realized. Charlie's goal since high school was to create and run a Star Trek themed coffee shop. He named it That Nebula, and had been successful so far. "You need to let your employees know what's going on."

"Adrian, babe, relax," he said. "You know I've got two people working today and we don't open for another hour or so." A town as small as Springfield didn't get much business at coffee places, so Charlie tended to keep his store closed until later in the day.

It had honestly become more of a hangout for high schoolers once they got off school. "I'll contact them once I'm off the phone to you and let them know what's going on, in case they don't already know."

"*Do* zombies drink coffee?" Adrian laughed, doing what she could to keep her spirits up a little longer.

"Isn't that a *Bailey School Kids* book?" Charlie said.

"I can't believe you just said that," she said flatly, still trying to hide the humor she found in his awful jokes every day. "Call your employees. I'll talk to you later."

She hung up and tried to relax. Charlie had never been the picture of perfect health, so obviously just because he had a headache didn't mean he would soon have a craving for human flesh. She just wished she could see him and know that he wasn't any more of a mess than he had been last night. She'd seen him in much worse conditions, but it was still always upsetting to see him in pain.

Adrian felt a bit better and calmer after talking to Charlie. She now realized how unlikely it was that he could become infected by simply sitting in a corner of their decrepit basement. She just wished she could figure out what it was that started the infection and how to make it go away. It was a bit ironic, however, thinking about how safe he probably was by just staying put. Did none of the people in those movies have a house with a basement? It was weird.

Being in the hallway wasn't doing very much

to make Adrian feel better, as she could hear Karl talking to Denise about how poorly she was doing as a leader. She was happy that she was walking with Nancy, but it was difficult to block out Karl's negative comments, even as she told Nancy about That Nebula.

Karl had started venting about Adrian before Denise had a chance to inform him that she sincerely didn't care about what he had to say. It wasn't difficult to process that he wasn't her biggest fan, but she was already feeling bad enough knowing that people she used to work with were either zombies, or had been killed by a coworker who had *turned into* a zombie. She had really wanted him to talk about what kind of reports he would have been giving this morning, or tell him all about the kind of exercises she enjoyed, and how often she did them.

After they'd gotten pretty far down the hall, Denise had to put a lot of work into ignoring the wretched stench of blood, feces and rotting flesh. She remembered hearing something about the fact that when a person dies, if there was any waste left in his or her body, it would all be expelled, which meant the zombies had now begun to not just change people, but kill them as well. While the zombies had completely devoured Hank's body, apparently some of the dead weren't quality enough for them to want. That was something the stories never discussed: just how picky are zombies? It seemed obvious that they tended to think fresh meat was better than meat that had been sitting for a while, getting cold and stale, but just how good did the brain have to be? Knowing that Lucy broke her vegan habits before she turned, though, maybe they *were* picky.

Nobody in the current party could help but notice puddles of liquid that were not far from where the fallen employees lay. It was easy to assume it was urine, never expecting that it was a substance known as cerebrospinal fluid, which the brain sits in when a person is healthy. To the zombies, it acted much like the juice in a steak: when it is too dry, eating it is not an enjoyable experience so they had no interest in feasting on those who no longer had this within their head.

Adrian and Charlie had often joked that if zombies were real, the two of them wouldn't have to worry: Charlie was constantly getting migraines and Adrian obviously had some type of brain issue, considering her sleep problem. And after seeing what they'd done to Hank, who had *documented* brain damage that affected almost every aspect of his life, this joke must have had no truth to it. She'd also never understood why the zombies always tended to prefer the brains of the living and not eat their own kind, no matter the circumstance. Obviously the zombies weren't not eating one another because they too had formed a team, but it seemed like they were able to move around and think to some extent. There must have been something still working inside of their heads.

As they made their way to the stairwell, deep in conversation about various topics, a few of them were talking about what life was like before this happened. Denise had shifted over to talking to Karl about how she had gotten the job as a reporter (interrupting him before he could get to any comments about how he, as a male, should be in charge), Nancy was telling Adrian about the time Natalie pulled a prank on her and gave her a caffeinated coffee with a late dinner, causing her to be up all night.

Adrian couldn't help but laugh; that was one time—try living with a sleeping condition. The entire experience reminded her of those old sleep sessions: trapped in a building, extremely worried, with a ton of angry people, no visitors allowed to come in, and everybody not in her group having some sort of medical issue. This realization creeped her out more than anything she'd suffered through so far. The day just kept getting better and better...

Nobody felt the need to talk once they'd gotten to the stairs, considering the zombies hadn't managed to open any doors let alone know how to walk on stairs.

"It really wasn't that hard to get this job," Denise continued. "I came in, read a few paragraphs on a sheet in my boldest but clearest voice, then went home. The next morning, a number I didn't recognize called my cell phone. I answered it, not even thinking that it might be this company, but it was Nathan. He told me that not only was I the best candidate who came in, but genuinely talented."

"That's actually impressive," Karl said. "Any idea how many people you were up against?" Having applied for the job as head news anchor, he'd had to wait quite a while before he found out if he'd gotten the job. There were supposedly about 8 other people who'd come in to read, but the job had gone to him. He'd been the only applicant who studied both journalism *and* media in college, but the chances he'd be the guy they chose was still 1 in 9. The anchor he was going to be replacing wasn't going to be leaving for another few weeks, so Nathan hadn't felt a huge amount of pressure choosing who he wanted. There hadn't been a lot of places close by that were looking for anyone in reporting, and this seemed like a great place to start. Of course, Karl couldn't have known at the time that the zombie apocalypse would be happening far before he could advance to a bigger news station.

Denise had no idea how many other applicants there had been, but she liked to think there were quite a few of them. They couldn't ask Nathan now.

At the bottom of the staircase, Adrian cracked open the door and peered through to check if they needed to start making noise again. She saw a few fairly normal looking beings shuffling around, mindlessly bumping into the walls and furniture. None of them looked like they were falling apart like the zombies she had seen standing outside of the building; these were either zombies or people trying to act like them so as not to attract any attention. Adrian made a mental note of the way they were behaving, wondering if any of it might help when they returned.

As the zombies weren't hiding from anything but instead seeking out flesh, they were not all put up in one area, but milling about anywhere possible. At last count, Adrian and her group had eight people (not including Charlie) and it was all too obvious that they were obscenely outnumbered. Although the zombies were generally avoiding them because of the noise they were making, they were everywhere. The number of zombies so overpowered the number of humans that it seemed this may be the new norm.

Ch. 14
Newsies

It's amazing how much a person's life can change in the course of one day. At this time yesterday, Adrian had already gotten off of work, and was at home making the brownies for today's potluck, waiting for Charlie so they could have their weekly date night. She could never have imagined that the events of today were going to happen; she would have suggested something other than their conventional zombie movie night if she knew. Yet here they were, discussing random topics on their way to the cafeteria, wondering if it still had anything to offer.

Adrian found a couple of empty boxes which they began to fill with as much food as they could carry: cans of beans, boxes of fruit saturated in sugary syrup that was supposed to be fruit juice, some off brand snack cakes, and several beverages that were blessedly still chilled. What Adrian would have done for a nice black coffee at the moment.

"I think that'll get us on for a little while, anyway," Adrian said, examining the contents of the boxes they'd filled. There wasn't a ton of food available, as the cafeteria didn't stay too well stocked. Knowing how 'TV dinner' the meals always were, most of the employees preferred to bring their own lunch, anyway. Generally in agreement, everybody picked up the box they'd filled and they headed back to the hallway to get back to Adrian's office, excited about what they'd scavenged.

"But wait," Denise realized, "what about the others in the building who haven't turned? We took *a lot* of what was in there, and there's always the chance of the electricity truly going out. Suppose they make the trek here, thinking they'll find a bunch of food."

"You make a good point, but judging by what we saw out there..." Adrian sighed, not wanting to admit what they all knew. "Judging by what we saw, there aren't a lot of us left. Remember when I was trying to form a team and you guys were among the only ones who believed me? I'm thinking those who've turned were the non-believers."

"But there could be—"

"I. Don't. Care," Adrian interrupted, suddenly aware that this trip hadn't done much in terms of improving anyone's mental well being. "Look Denise, I understand what you're saying and where the issue lays, but anyone who's still alive can pretty much assume we'll be in my office and can find us when they want help."

She then addressed the group as a whole. "Bathroom break: who needs it?" The bathroom break this time posed a different issue as this group was slightly different from the one earlier, and

Denise didn't like Karl being in the bathroom when she was going to use it.

Given the fact that they'd already lost two people who didn't need to die, Adrian told Denise that she wasn't going to make him stand in the hallway just because he was the only one there who was a man. Nobody else took issue with the fact that he was there.

When all the women were finished, Adrian offered Karl to use the toilet.

"This has been uncomfortable enough with just you guys," was his response. "Your solution to this issue earlier works much better for me." Since everybody was so keen on getting back to Adrian's office without anyone turning, they ventured back into the hallway, still carrying their boxes of food.

"Nancy, we're going to get you and Natalie back together," Adrian said, completely out of the blue. Nancy didn't know what to say, or if she even should, so she waited until Adrian went on. "I've been thinking about how important it is to me that I get back with Charlie and make sure he's alright. From everything you've said, you and Natalie are just as important to each other as he and I are to each other." She'd never dream of ending a sentence in a preposition. "It's really not fair of me to put all of this weight on getting Charlie back and only mildly plan on doing anything about you and her."

"You are a wonderful human being," Nancy responded, trying to process what she was being told. They still had a fair amount of ground to cover before they were back in Adrian's office, so she

decided it was the time to share everything about why she and Natalie had been together and stayed together for so long, aside from the "living in Springfield" thing. Adrian had long thought that those two should write a book on relationships, but Nancy's thing had never really been writing.
"It's better than being a wonderful zombie being. Yeah, go ahead and tell me." Everybody at News Sun really only knew that Nancy was in a relationship with another female and had been getting ready to propose to her. Nancy ended up telling Adrian everything, even what had led her to ask Natalie out in the first place: she'd been dating Natalie's twin brother, Scott, for a few months and he wanted her to meet his family. He'd set it up to be super low stress, simply taking her over to his house. Immediately after meeting her, Nancy developed a crush on Scott's sister, but didn't really worry about it. She had already come to terms with the fact that she was bisexual and figured it wouldn't be an issue to continue dating him. She ended up developing a friendship, so she spent about as much time with Natalie as she did with Scott.

Nancy and Natalie were best friends, so of course Nancy got invited to the family celebration of Natalie's birthday at a nice Italian restaurant. She drove there with Scott, who explained she'd be meeting the rest of the family who'd gotten there about fifteen minutes previous.

The second Nancy walked in and saw Natalie, sitting at the head of the table, she realized she was in love with her. There was no use denying that she felt any emotion towards her best friend other than love. It was incredibly uncomfortable, and she argued with herself the entire night, telling herself that the love she was feeling was actually towards Scott, but by the end of the night, she had to stop pretending.

When she broke up with Scott the next day, he asked if it was because she was in love with someone else. After he'd gotten her to admit that, yes, she was in love with another person, he pulled out his phone and called his sister, much to Nancy's dismay.

"I'll let her tell you the rest of the story when we pick her up," Nancy said, smirking. Adrian was actually fully invested in the story, which (she realized) was probably why Nancy had even done that. She also realized that, having been so invested in listening to that history, she hadn't had to bother with being as scared as she rationally should have, and they were just approaching her office door.

Everything seemed the same as they walked up to the door. Except that what they had assumed to be Nathan's corpse was no longer there. Adrian actively decided not to even think about that until (*if*) they encountered him as a zombie. It was equally likely that he was a zombie as that a zombie had gotten him. Not their problem at the time.

Inside the room, everything was the same, which was great. Adrian didn't see Nick right off, but realized it was because he'd crawled under her desk, apparently overwhelmed at the prospect of having to just sit quietly until the other group came back with food. Raleigh appeared to be talking to him, trying to convince him to come out.

"This is just our situation now," Raleigh was saying as they approached the desk to put the boxes on top of it. She was talking in a calming, silky voice. Adrian had always been impressed with how therapists were able to keep their head on straight, no matter what the situation, and was glad that somebody else was dealing with Nick. "We have our fearless leader, Adrian, we're all safe and secluded from the zombies outside, and we're on the way to figuring out what caused this, which will become figuring out how to fight them and avoid ourselves getting infected." Raleigh's change in composure made it seem as though she'd struck a chord with him.

"And then we get to stab them all?" came his hopeful voice.

"We're going to do what Adrian thinks is safest," Raleigh answered, gently. It impacted Adrian a bit, with how much weight the counselor had put on the fact that she was everybody's hope to get out of this, as if she knew everything there was to know about surviving the apocalypse. Sure, she'd seen all the movies, enjoyed watching the classic "person falling as they're running for their life" trope, been fascinated by the few times the source of infection *was* identified, but it felt so different when it was *you*, in *your* actual life. She'd enjoyed it immensely, but was coming to realize that by watching these films she was really just engaging in *Schadenfreude*; enjoying watching others get hurt. Not even a month ago, she and Charlie had gone to a theater that was doing a special screening of the original *Night of the Living Dead.*

Pushing aside the very real idea that they were doomed, Adrian bent down to confirm what Raleigh had just said, in an attempt to keep morale up. "She's right. We've already been establishing how we can survive in this building, the mission to get food was successfully accomplished, and you really seem like your normal self so far." Raleigh could tell that Nick had been in a weird headspace all day, but this wasn't the right time to mention that. They needed privacy from the others.

"We got food?" he asked, the tension in his muscles beginning to ease up. Adrian grabbed the first thing she saw from the closest box (a fruit cup) and showed it to him, so he would know they weren't just making it up to make him feel better.

Linda, Denise, and Trevor had already started taking everything out of the boxes and organizing them based on what could go bad, versus the classic "you know that bomb shelter you have? Yeah, keep these food items there."

They were in the middle of a fairly heated debate on or not the fruit cups should go with "eat these soon" or "these will last for years" when there was a frantic knock on the door.

Adrian looked out the small, rectangular window on her office door to see somebody who she didn't recall seeing at the picnic. This woman had a look of sheer terror, and clearly wanted to be let in. Although the decay process the zombies went through was fairly rapid and whoever this was still looked alive, there had been no established way of saying, "I'm alive, let me in." Adrian took the chance and opened the door.

"Who are you?" Adrian asked. Not only had this woman not been at the picnic, but Adrian sincerely could not remember seeing her around the office, ever. "Were you outside when all of this started, or always in this building?"

"My name is... I'm... I work in human resources and I know a little bit about zombies, okay?" she said, her nervousness suddenly becoming anger.

Adrian tried to make a joke. "What, do you have an embarrassing name or something?" Seeing the woman's face after she'd said this, it became clear that that was true. "Oh! I'm sorry. Uh, let's.. Um okay. Let me introduce you to the crew: I'm Adrian, that's Trevor, he's Karl, she's Nancy, that's Denise, Nick's the one in the fetal position, Raleigh is our counselor right now but you probably knew her, and that's Linda. I've become sort of a leader because I love *(loved)* zombie literature, Raleigh is still working as a counselor, and we just came back with some food, have you eaten?"

"Are you a writer for the paper, or—"

"No, I was an editor." Nameless Employee didn't seem to have reverted to everything normal now being past tense. She should have phrased it, "Were you a writer for the paper" as there was no paper any longer. Life was different. "Why does that matter to you, oh One With An Embarrassing Name?"

"You just used a pretty major run on sentence. And look, if my name's about to be 'one with an embarrassing name' I guess I'll just tell you: it's not that my name is *embarrassing,* it's just... my family history isn't that fun. We're related to someone who was in the Battle of Gettysburg and my mom is rather proud of it. Teresa. My name is Teresa because that was the wife of Daniel Sickles, who was actually a rather bad man. I have no idea why my parents chose to keep the family name." Adrian broke out laughing. Not because it was a bad name, but because she had expected something much worse.

"It's not a zombie story without a person with an odd name now, is it?" she laughed. "Well welcome to the clan. Come on over to my desk and I'll let you know everything we've figured out so far."

She took Teresa up to her desk where they had all of the information down on the whiteboard. It looked like the group had worked out the issue with the fruit cups by just putting an even amount of them in both piles.

As she was explaining what they knew to Teresa, it became clear that Teresa was incredibly smart. She had not only already figured all of this out, but also she was still alive.

"How did you come to learn all of this?" Adrian had to know.

"Well I was trapped out there, unaware that there was a group of you that had not been infected, just sort of checking everywhere I could to see if there was a group like this one. And when you're on your own, you do come to learn what will help you stay alive. To be honest, I'm kind of surprised you didn't hear me; I was making *a lot* of noise."

"Well at least you found us and realized as much as you did." This survivor seemed to have her act together considerably more than any of the others in the room. Adrian deemed it necessary and useful to tell her what the ultimate plan was for the group.

For the first time in a while, things started looking up; if Teresa had managed to stay with such high hopes after being alone in the hallway of such a small building, there was obviously hope for them all. The rest of the survivors were still getting excited over all of the food they'd brought back and paying no attention to the two at the desk.

"I'll cut you a deal," Adrian said, reminding herself of a couple of the characters in gangster movies she'd seen.

"What's that?" Teresa asked.

"I trust many of these people less than I did this morning when I came into work and don't want to tell them my ultimate plan. You, however, are still on my good side. If you can keep this a secret, I will tell no one what your real name is: we're really about to start a new life and I'm the only one who knows it. And you said you worked in..."

"Human resources, right. I know none of these people so they wouldn't know the truth. Nathan kind of liked to pretend my department wasn't a thing. To him, we were information technology level employees."

"Which is why you weren't at the picnic. Got it. Okay, but before I introduce you to them, what do you want to be called?" It was clear that Teresa had thought about this many times before as she took no time responding, "Caroline." A fan of the author E.F. Benson, she just blurted the first name from one of his stories she could think of.

"Alright. Caroline it is. Your old name is gone, now let's go meet everyone who's in here," Adrian agreed. She was secretly jealous that this person got to change her name: Adrian was named after the town both of her parents grew up in (not even where they met), and she just thought the rest of her team's names were dull. Then again, maybe they had cool stories behind how they got their name: Karl may be named after a guy in a band or something, perhaps Linda was named after someone who'd had an impact on her parents, Nancy's parents could have been obsessed with the Nancy Drew series. There were infinite possibilities.

128

Ch. 15
Broadcast News

"So how are we doing over here?" Adrian asked, interrupting the food sorting.

"I'd say good," Raleigh said as everybody shrugged and nodded in agreement. "It looks like there's enough food to last at least over a week. You did great, away team." Adrian was surprisingly proud of her leadership skills that had shone through on the trip and used that feeling to introduce their newest recruit.

"Not to interrupt the celebration, but we've got a new helper," she said boldly. "Everybody please welcome... Caroline. She's been in the hallway going through what we've gone through in here and I swear she's healthy."

"Hey y'all," she said, dropping all previous formalities she might have had to worry about. All at once, everybody started talking. There seemed to be no general agreement that it was safe to add Caroline to the group. Admittedly, none of them had assumed they'd encounter another living human, and it felt to some of them that somehow the zombies had evolved to looking and acting like they were still alive. Among those who disagreed with this, Adrian caught some of the things people were saying: "She doesn't *look* great", "I mean...", "So we're dead."

Denise's voice rang out above all others. "What's next, boss?"

"I wanted to look at what we should have been reporting on today," Adrian answered. "I know I had to check up on the sports news, but what else was there?"

She sat at her desk and glared at the Dismember Me Zombie that Charlie had gotten her for their one year marriage anniversary, sitting on the edge of her desk. It seemed to mock her. She'd set it there on the day she got this office and would always glance at it if she needed a slight pick-me-up. Now it only served as a reminder of the fact that she, her husband, and everybody she ever loved were ultimately doomed.

"Well, Nathan had me talking about the cloud formations in the sky to prove that fall is coming right on schedule," Karl said—a repeat (if more in depth) of the news Adrian had heard this morning.

"Yeah, I had that as well," Nancy agreed, referring to the notes she'd printed out. "And then there was the usual fluff stories he always made us cover, today focusing on a corgi who'd produced a litter of two more puppies than they usually have."

"Typical," Adrian muttered. Any time the other station was showing what the boss considered to be useless news stories, he would dig around for any type of news that was even mildly interesting. It was all very biased as well: just because Nathan thought it was cool did not necessarily mean their viewers would enjoy it. Of course, none of that mattered now, as they were just trying to survive and might never go on the air again.

Every time Adrian had to go in for monitoring as a child, she would get to the point of exhaustion that she would go a little... unhinged. She knew she'd be at that point fairly soon. The way she looked at it, she could either talk to Raleigh—who probably had enough people unloading how they were feeling onto her—or suggest that she and some of the others who weren't doing well start taking short naps. It was getting to be about five o'clock at this point, the time she and her husband had planned on leaving for the family picnic and also the time she'd get tired on a normal day.

"Alright gang," she announced, "here's the deal: I know a lot of us are getting testy because we've seen what's going on out there and know we're in danger. Lucy wasn't a one-off. There are legitimate zombies in the hallway. Obviously, the away mission did next to nothing for us aside from getting some food, so I'm thinking we should start taking maybe 30 minute naps while the others keep watch. I'm sure my office floor isn't *incredibly* comfortable, but I'm totally drifting off and figure you might be also." She looked directly at Karl as she said this. "I honestly don't see us getting out of this building any time soon, we'll be here likely all night unless some rescue team comes for us, so..."

With this realization, everyone was on board with her idea, letting her first choose where she wanted to lay down. Everyone agreed that the away team deserved to get a break first, although Caroline was allowed to join them as well.

Adrian Chase had rarely experienced a good night's rest and as she attempted to drift off, she tried to convince herself that everything happening was an effect of that: Lucy hadn't murdered somebody, Hank hadn't committed suicide, and they were all still at the picnic enjoying the dishes people had brought in.

The moment she closed her eyes, though, all she could do was become hyper alert, listening for scraping at the door or possible movement next to her and she saw Hank's mangled body in her mind's eye. She convinced herself that although the nap may result in nightmares, they couldn't be any worse than the world she was living in now.

She somehow managed to nod off, waking up feeling slightly better than she'd been before falling asleep. Once she was awake, however, she found that not only had she only been down for twenty of her allotted thirty minutes, but she had forty texts and five calls missed from her husband. The drowsiness left in Adrian immediately drained out of her body as she bolted up and called him back.

"Charlie," she gasped when he picked up in the middle of the first ring. "Are you okay?"

"Yeah," he replied, noting that she sounded low on air. "Why are you talking like that?"

"Some of us have started taking short naps," she explained, still talking low. "That's why I wasn't answering."

"And you were one of them? So basically what you're telling me is that you, Adrian Chase, can only sleep well in the case of a zombie apocalypse?"

"I'm thinking better now, if that's what you mean," she told him, trying not to laugh at this realization as everyone else was still sleeping. "But yeah, that's essentially what I'm saying. How are things on your end?"

"Not the greatest," he replied. "It's lonely. You're the only one I've been talking to. I realized I really can't call any of the parents because they'd think we're crazy. I've been trying to distract myself from the fact that I've been alone all day and very possibly may always be by—"

And suddenly something was triggered in Adrian and she once again couldn't keep her head about her.

"Adrian, hon, you okay?" he asked, sensing this.

"No," she said, acknowledging the lingering feeling she'd had all day but trying to silence that she was crying. "I should have wished you a good day this morning. I didn't because of the picnic we should have gone to, I didn't know it might have been my last chance to see you in person."

"Adrian, it'll be okay," he said. "If I can promise you anything, it's that we'll see each other again. And soon. You said they didn't like noise, right? If we can ignore the psychological damage it will cause me, I can always plug in those new speakers I got and go outside to the car, still blaring music, and drive to your building."

"As lovely as that would be... please don't worry about it. This has changed me. I don't think I'm the same person I was this morning and I don't want you to change too." She didn't go too into detail, as her fear was that he may not love who she'd become anymore although she knew she'd love him no matter what. Sure, killing in self defense was different than killing for no reason, but she still wasn't at all proud of what she'd have to do. "We've locked the doors, anyway, and I don't think anyone would want to open them back up."

"*Please* don't leave your office," he said. "If you stay put, so will I."

"We've got provisions," she said, looking around. "Call me if anything changes."

She felt arguably more emotional than she had before the call. How could she have not said goodbye to him this morning? She was constantly telling him how much she loved him, but not enough to wake him up for two seconds? The hatred she felt towards herself for making that absolutely mindless decision, for never even considering that some type of negative thing could happen to herself or her husband overpowered her in the worst possible way.

Thankfully or not, Raleigh picked up on how she was doing and asked if she needed to talk.

"I'm still in my corner, but I'll call you in an hour. I love you."

"Love you, too. Bye."

Ch. 16
The Social Network

After explaining what she'd done (or not done) that morning, Raleigh repeated exactly what Adrian already knew: there was no way to have known what was going to happen that day, and how unlikely it was that Charlie was infected. Of course at this point it was less about either of them getting infected than about never seeing each other again. If he never left the house or she the office, then there was no chance of them ever connecting again. And what if the zombies evolved to learn to climb stairs, knock down doors or break glass? It was all probable in Adrian's mind.

By the time their mini session was over, it was time for the first group to be woken and the second group to sleep. As expected, Karl cursed at the employee who woke him but got up anyway, sure to be moodier than before, and now complaining of hunger. They decided that one group would eat while the others slept. Adrian and the others looked at the chart the sleepers had made explaining who got what food per day and divvied up their first meals as temporary survivors of a zombie attack. As they ate, they quietly discussed how they were feeling and what their next move might be. Adrian and Caroline seemed most interested in helping out with the process, both being much less upset than the others who were now awake.

"Okay since we're such a small group, I'm going to say this," Adrian sighed, partly worried about the others finding out that she did this, partly upset that Karl was in this group. "We may be locked in, but I want us to get out. Yes we're locked in and others are locked out, but us being in means the infected are as well. Sure they *might* slow down without feeding, but there are so many here that they'll probably survive for a while. I mean, for all we know the zombies may become desperate enough to feed on each other. We don't know how these things work in real life. And I'm confident that they'll eventually figure out how to get in here, be it with strength or some form of intelligence. We can't win by trapping them and hiding out in here. At some point, we'll run out of food, and the zombies that are in the building might not be killed easily. It makes more sense to get out of this building, as if that happens, we'll be stuck forever with no chance of escape." She got it: everybody felt safe where they were, but if they had any way to live into their seventies at the least, they couldn't spend those remaining 20 to 30 years here.

"We need another group to go cut the power in the building. They can use the dim light provided by cell phones and the fish tanks in the hallway. And when it gets dark tonight, we'll get out. These zombies don't give a fuck about light but hate sound and *possibly* dark."

For a quick moment she fantasized about no zombies in the building but just the uninfected and her husband, creating a new society, all uninfected, aware of what caused this and able to keep the cause away. It was a pleasing, borderline orgasmic thought, and she had to push it out of her head knowing that it wasn't going to happen or if it was, it wouldn't be any time soon.

"Can anyone think of someone who might still be around the building?" She thought of Hank, wishing he was an option, trying to accept the fact that he was dead. Reminding herself that everybody had undoubtedly lost someone in this mess, she pushed Hank out of her mind, focusing on what they still had.

A sudden chorus of moans right outside the door made her wish she had a way to communicate with the zombies: it seemed like they had their own way to communicate which may have had its own grammar rules. Or maybe it was similar to how you can tell what's going on with a dog based on the sorts of sounds it made. If they were the same as dogs, these zombies must have been not only hungry but pissed that they couldn't find anyone or anything to feed on. Considering just how upset and insistent to get in they seemed, this group had to have been the only living, non-undead things in the building.

Adrian pinned herself to the door of her office, hoping that they hadn't developed the super strength of some of the zombies in literature who could break glass like it was tissue paper. Once again paralyzed with fear, this time to the extent that her whole body was shaking, she peered out the foggy and bloody window to see if she could identify those trying to get in.

Judging by the uniform (if torn up and caked with blood) the current wannabe intruder was decked out in, the janitor was one of the unlucky bunch. Or lucky, given that, if uninfected, he would have to clean all of the blood and bodies that had accumulated around the building. And he wasn't alone: along with the janitor was what functionality was left of Nathan (slow for a zombie), someone Caroline confirmed had worked in the cubicle next to her in HR, and (Adrian was beyond horrified to see) Lucy bringing up the rear obviously having attacked far more of the living than anyone else in the group judging by the amount of fresh and dried blood she was drenched in.

She was amazed to see that none of these were children, thinking maybe they got out of the building before any of them turned. That would be amazing news. Still, no matter how bad their situation got, it could always get worse. Much, much worse. Psychologically, physically, it could always get worse. And with half the room asleep and the other half too scared to do *anything*, these zombies weren't going away any time soon. It now truly occurred to Adrian that the majority of the building must have been infected; finding Caroline uninfected was a blessing and was not likely to happen again.

A few of those who were sleeping began stirring and all who were awake hoped they would have it together well enough to input some advice. Adrian wasn't about to back down on her plan to get out of the room by nightfall even with this new scare because she knew that just because they were hiding and not getting infected, it was really doing nothing for them. Their mental state was almost as important as their physical being and she wanted to be able to keep her team both healthy *and* happy.

The first one awake, Trevor asked what everybody was doing, frozen in front of the door. A quick glance outside answered his question, seeing a couple zombies banging their heads on the window, trying to break the glass that was keeping them safe inside the office. Realizing those inside weren't doing too well, Trevor stood up and walked to the door where he started banging back on the glass to make twice as much noise as the zombies. It didn't take long for them to begin shuffling away, looking for others to feast upon who were not as noisy.

"Thanks, Trevor," Adrian said watching the zombies retreating down the hallway. There were two fish tanks in her hall and she watched as the janitor and the guy from HR avoided them but also noticed that they didn't seem to bother Lucy or Nathan. That seemed noteworthy, as the rest of them seemed to be doing everything they could to stay at least three feet away.

"How are you doing?" he asked, genuinely concerned.

"I've been better," she answered. "But I've also been worse. And you?"

Trevor shrugged.

"I mean, I guess I'm doing about the same as you, but there's a lot more pressure being put on you," he said. "It seems like Caroline's helping a lot, right?"

"Yeah," Adrian agreed. "It was pretty bleak before she showed up (and it still is) but if she could survive on her own for as long as she did out there, it seems just slightly more hopeful now. Right?"

"I think you're right about that," Trevor said, feeling the same way. "Do you have to call Charlie again, or..."

"Nah, I just talked to him. And I honestly don't think I should keep contacting him, considering the migraine he had last night. He needs rest."

"We... we don't think he's infected, right?" Trevor made sure. "Migraines are normal for your guy?" Adrian nodded, starting to think the migraine might have been his sixth sense foreshadowing this event, similar to how nervous she'd been over seemingly nothing, hours ago.

"Alright, so what do we do after these guys wake up?" Adrian didn't want to leave the room until nightfall, given that the darkness would be pure in that case, but before creating a plan she realized, "You work in the building's IT department, right?"

"Yeah, what of it?"

"The tanks. Of fish. The tanks with the fish in them. The fish tanks. What happens if they get turned off?" Ignoring Adrian's just becoming a human thesaurus, he answered that really all it meant was that the tanks would at some point need to be cleaned. Nothing bad would happen to the fish, it would just get a little *"Finding Nemo* at the dentist's office". Discovering that the fish wouldn't die and would still make the zombies avoid their tanks was (quite literally) a life saver. She didn't know why the zombies were avoiding the tanks: it could have been the water, something about plants within it, but hopefully not the sound of the filter going, since that wouldn't happen once the power was cut. With any luck, the lights in the tanks being out would get the zombies to run into them. She didn't know what would happen if they did, but it was something to keep her going.

142

Ch. 17
Tomorrow Never Dies

After the second group's nap, they were given their daily share of food. Adrian realized that they were all faring much better than some groups in the stories she had read, which she realized was one of the many ways reality is weirder than fiction. A hotel room with a minibar of alcoholic beverages, overpriced water and salted peanuts was nothing compared to the cafeteria food they'd managed to snatch up. Plus, their group was large and all in one place.

There was little to no talking as the second group, now awake, was eating and the others were still shook up by the attack they'd just survived. Since the servings were so scarce, however, their dining was quickly finished and it was only silent for a short while.

"So there was another attack?" Raleigh said, noting the crimson red dripping on the window.

"Yeah," Adrian said. *That one* was scary, though. Everyone's alright for now, yes?" As there were no complaints issued, she went on, "So it's only, what, 6:49 right now? Not the time most people go to bed?"

Everybody found themselves suddenly wishing it wasn't fall but summer, so it would at least still be light outside.

"That being said, we'll all leave to kill the power once it's late. I know the danger we'll be putting ourselves in, and I know you know it too, but there's strength in numbers and I'll feel safer knowing we're all together and that you know what's happening with all of us. You can amuse yourself in whatever way you see fit until then."

On a normal day, a command like that would have seen Adrian pulling out whatever zombie novel she was rereading at the moment, but given their situation she decided to have another conversation with Caroline.

"How long were you out there?" she asked. "Avoiding them."

"A few hours," Caroline said with a shrug. Given how passive she was about the fact that she'd just been roaming around in zombie infested hallways, it was clear that she hadn't exactly comprehended how dangerous the situation was.

"Okay how about this: do you realize just how screwed we are?"

"Well sure, but if I could stay safe out there and you've all been in here..."

"But we don't know how it all started. We

could all be infected and just not yet showing the symptoms; you weren't here earlier but one of our crew had it and didn't know until later."

"You should sit," Caroline said. "Sit here, I'll be right back." Adrian was up for anything that would make her feel marginally better, so did as she was told. Caroline went to her desk and put the toy zombie into the drawer.

"Out of sight, out of mind," she said. "Now to do something about that awful window there."

Adrian had a sense that Caroline was trying to take over her role as their leader, a position she admittedly hadn't wanted in the beginning, but she wasn't ready to give it up. She had been hesitant to be the new hope for the group, but she'd adjusted quickly and thought she'd been doing a pretty decent job. And it was kind of fun. She let it be for the moment, given her lack of skills during their last attack, but wasn't going to stand for it too long.

Adrian didn't know if it was the stress of their situation or actually caring what happened, but she thanked Caroline for the help.

"I should be okay soon, though," she added. "Then we'll get back on track."

"Well yeah," Caroline said. "I wasn't about to get behind the wheel of this crazy train. Uh, do you have tape in any of these drawers?" There was always a roll of duct tape in the first drawer in her desk (it had been there when she moved into the office) which Adrian had no trouble locating. Sitting next it, she found a bottle of hand sanitizer that would at least serve to keep the occupants of the room *slightly* more clean.

As she was handing the roll over to Caroline, it occurred to her that this may be a mistake; Caroline might have a plan to tie her up with the tape that she was currently surrendering. She hesitated for a moment, considering how difficult it would be to get out of a duct tape straight jacket, but ended up deciding that if Caroline made a move to do that, she would know beforehand and be able to move her arms enough that the task couldn't be accomplished. And anyway, that was just her being paranoid; it wasn't totally unlike how Hank used to think Lucy would react to him trying to be her friend.

Caroline was still of a very sound mind, however, and only asked for the tape to cover up the window now covered in red and black blood.

It was nice for the rest of the team to not be forced to see that, although some of them couldn't help but worry about the fact that they weren't completely aware of what was going on outside now.

"That's perfect," Adrian said once the window was fully covered. She had worried that they would end up breaking the glass, but now she pictured a zombie breaking the glass and then its hand getting stuck on the tape. It was stressful, though, not seeing out the small window, not knowing if a zombie was about to pound on the door. When the window hadn't been covered, she'd seen them before any sort of knocking happened, but now it would come as a shock. And with everyone already so on edge, it would be more shocking to them all.

The window being blocked off gave the room a completely different vibe. On normal days, her door was almost always open, allowing people to come and go as they needed. She always knew what was going on in the hall. All day, she'd used the small window as a surrogate for that, always knowing the ongoings in that hallway, which now she could see none of.

Upon thinking about that window, she realized it would be good to put the blind over her window that looked out on the parking lot downstairs.

As hard as she tried not to, she stole a glance at the outside; maybe now there were only zombies in the building. Maybe something in the ink had caused all of this and nobody outside was infected for more than an hour or two. But no. There were hordes of infected *outside* of the building as well. She flashed back to what it was like entering the building today, completely unaware that her day was going to be headed south to the extent that it had.

She was relieved to notice they weren't making much progress getting into the building. It seemed like the mob couldn't quite digest that they should all work together if they hoped to ever get in. Random trios of them slamming their full force into the concrete and glass separating those inside from the ones outside was doing them no good.

"I hate life," Adrian muttered.

She couldn't get the image of those zombies out of her mind. They formed an entire pack surrounding the front door of the building. She would have done anything to be in a slightly more secure location. Sure, she knew that the doors and front of the building were nearly impenetrable, but the thought of them starting to work as a team wormed its way into her head and she had to keep herself from panicking.

She got into the exact pattern she used to use trying to get to sleep, and suddenly could understand why the doctors told her to do this: although her heart was still beating as fast as if she'd just been jogging, there was something relaxing about focusing on nothing but her breathing. Of course, given that her issue with sleep was something other than having too many things on her mind, it had done nothing to help with that problem. But today she discovered that once you've given up on surviving, the possibility of sleep came *much* easier.

Ch. 18
Shattered Glass

Continuing to take in the scene, Adrian noticed how far the bodies were from the guts spilling out of them. She didn't know if the zombies decided the guts weren't good enough to eat or they simply got off on slicing open a living thing's stomach and watching it writhe until it slowed to a stop. She cringed at the thought and realized they really did have to figure out how to stop them as opposed to simply slowing them down as they did with zombie-Nathan.

In the books and movies Adrian used to enjoy, there would always be that heroic moment in which someone admitted he or she was proficient in shooting a gun at a moving target and, oh hey, yeah also I have a sidearm stowed away under the creaky floorboard in the other room. This was not a book or movie, though.

"I have a *staple* gun in my office," Karl offered

once Adrian voiced this thought process.

"At this point I'm willing to try anything," Adrian said with a shrug. "How far away are you?" Adrian hadn't learned where any of her coworkers' offices were because she'd never really needed to visit them. Sure she knew where Hank and Nathan worked but they were more personal to her than anyone else in the building.

"I'm *lit-e-rally* two doors down," he said, motioning with his hands on the word "literally". "It's not a big deal; I can go alone..."

Of everyone in their party, Karl seemed to have digested their situation least; of course they weren't going to let him venture out alone. He needed someone to lead and another to watch behind them. And if he wasn't taking it seriously, then of course he wouldn't be on his guard to the extent that the others were.

"C'mere," Adrian said to him. "Come here and look out that window then tell me you still want to go by yourself."

He looked out the window to see exactly what Adrian had been looking at moments before, finally starting to understanding their situation. In order to try to cover up the stupidity of what he just suggested, he cleared his throat nervously and suggested perhaps one or two of them go with him.

"It's almost 8," Adrian said to herself once Karl and the two he chose to walk with him were gone. "We've survived for about eight hours with flesh eating monsters in the hallways. It's not much in the grand scheme of things, but it's... well it's far longer than we'd survived a zombie apocalypse yesterday."

"What are you saying?" Linda asked.

"Oh, hey Linda," Adrian said, returning to reality. "No, I was just psyching myself up. It's crazy that this group of us have made it this long and I'm just reminding myself of the fact."

"We can *do* this," Linda assured her, placing her hand on Adrian's back for comfort. "Everyone is aware of the plan and going to do exactly what you say."

"Thanks, Linda," she said, now feeling a bit more confident about what they were about to do.

"How are you doing, anyway?" Thinking of everything she'd seen over the course of the past few hours, Adrian had to answer that she wasn't all that great. She was completely overwhelmed thinking about all the people they'd lost, trying not to consider friends she had out in the world who were probably becoming infected, wondering if and how this could all be ended, and (although she'd never say it out loud) sincerely wondering what it's like to just give up and become a zombie. The zombies didn't seem to show any fear, but by giving in and becoming one of them, she would ultimately become the enemy.

What was it like to be a zombie? To have that craving for human flesh, a craving that was not only beyond the most twisted minds, but that the company vegetarian and vegan now had?

The closest thing she could imagine it would be like was how it felt realizing just how much she loved Charlie: she'd just started college and was only a few weeks into it. She'd never really had an interest in getting intimate with anyone she had dated in the past, but suddenly realized she really, really wanted to lose her virginity to him. It wasn't even that she no longer wished to be a virgin, but that the idea of doing it with Charlie and Charlie only was incredibly appealing to her, when she had never wanted anything even close to it with him or anybody else. While she had had crushes on celebrities like everyone does, she'd never thought about hooking up with them, but suddenly the idea of hooking up with Charlie had been something she not only wanted, but absolutely *needed*.

The feeling of finally getting hold of the flesh and brains the undead clearly so desperately desired couldn't have been so different from when Adrian finally got what she wanted. Considering how maddeningly curious Adrian was about all of this, she decided she should talk to Raleigh before they went out. Unfortunately she was one of the two who went with Karl, so she decided to rest until until the party got back.

Ch. 19
All the President's Men

Adrian stayed this way for around ten minutes, thankful that nobody interrupted her attempt to relax. The first thing to come to her mind was not only the horde, but a song she used to enjoy about a zombie asking politely to eat somebody's brain. A kid she'd had a crush on in high school had introduced her to it as she never was good at hiding her love of zombies. A love that was quickly diminishing the longer she had to hide with her coworkers in her cramped one room office.

"Won't be long until sunset," she announced to the room once she had gathered herself again. "We're going to venture out soon; is anybody genuinely not feeling well?" She asked not so much because she worried that they were mentally unstable, but rather that she would have those ones go first as they may be infected too. She cringed, for one because that was a really cold blooded thought for her to have, but also because, honestly, if anyone were to become infected, she'd prefer it to be herself so she wouldn't have to deal with experiencing anyone else turning, or the rest of her life in this apocalypse.

It was a relief to know that they were all feeling like their normal selves, although unfortunate as that meant they had no obvious scouting party.

Adrian went on to explain the plan: pick a walking buddy, make sure you get to know them well enough to know if they get the infection. It was time to go to the basement. She stood aside and watched as everybody paired off until she was left with Nancy.

Although it was dark out by the time everyone had his or her buddy, nobody was ready to leave yet.

"Look," Adrian explained, "if we are going to do anything positive here, I firmly believe that we shouldn't leave this room until it's not just dark, but also late. I'm perfectly comfortable with most or even all of us sleeping until midnight. The zombies will likely be bored by then, listlessly roaming around, avoiding fish tanks, maybe even slowing down."

She avoided admitting that she was trying to get *some* kind of zombie cliché into this situation, given that nothing much had presented itself in the same way that it was in her stories: noise usually attracted them, it never came from seemingly heathy people, and nobody in those movies knew anything about surviving this apocalypse. Generally by this point, the zombies would have broken down the door and the survivors would have some way to truly exterminate them.

The events of the day *had* exhausted everyone, and they all agreed that this was the best possible plan. It didn't seem important for any of them to stay up guarding the door, being that the zombies were yet to figure out how doors worked. Again Adrian got first pick on where she wanted to sleep and the others were stuck figuring out how to fit themselves onto the crowded floor. Adrian sent Charlie a text letting him know that he wouldn't be hearing from her for a while because they were going to get some rest, and she set an alarm to wake them up at around 1:30, hoping that the power would stay on and her phone wouldn't die.

As Adrian lay waiting for sleep to find her, she could hear the soft breathing of everyone in the room. Someone (who she had to assume was Karl) was snoring fairly loudly. Reminding herself she only had a few hours to get refreshed, she tried to find a comfortable position, thought about her husband who was undoubtedly also trying to fall asleep, and eventually fell into a deep, dreamless sleep.

A beeping sound at exactly 1:30 AM woke Adrian and the others up from their slumbers. She could hear several of them groaning in protest, coming out of whatever world they'd just been in and adjusting to being back in one that had real life zombies.

"Um, how is everyone feeling?" Adrian asked timidly, feeling about the same as those who would rather not have been awoken. Trevor seemed the only one who was fully rested, which made Adrian suspicious that perhaps *he* had been the one snoring away that whole time. Standing up from her spot on the floor, Adrian flipped on the lights, much to the protest of the others in the room.

"Sorry guys, but we really have to start figuring out how we're going to get to the fuse box to shut off the power." Ironic, she realized, as in any book she'd read, nature would have taken care of that already. Obviously nobody who worked at electric companies had turned into zombies quite yet. And anyway, it was the beginning of the month, so power wouldn't shut off due to missed payments for at least 30 days.

"She's right," Caroline said, standing up. "We can't go out there with no weapons and just assume that being loud is going to keep us safe. Who has a cell phone?"

Several of those still sitting pulled out phones from his or her pocket. "Okay, if you have a flashlight app, have it up and ready to go. If you don't, get one. The internet should still be working."

"I have a question," Nancy said. "What if the government knows what's going on and is sending people to save us? Should we not leave the power on and stay in one place?" After seeing the detritus the outside world had already become, this idea hit Adrian as risible, but she forced herself to hold in the laugh she could feel rising up her throat. They hadn't seen what she had that was trying to get in the building. She had heard rumors back in the day that the government had a plan in the case of a zombie apocalypse, but she didn't think they would start at a small office building in downtown Springfield. On top of that, in classical zombie lore, it was often the government's doing.

"I see your point, but if they are coming for us, we need to do everything we can to still be alive and healthy by the time they get here," she instead replied. "And I think that this will help us do that."

"What if our phones die?" Denise asked. "We won't have a way to recharge them if the power's out."

"That's a good question," Adrian said. "I really liked Caroline's idea about having our cell phones out for a light source, and I think if one or two of us left our phones powered off in my office, we can get through this with just that."

"You've been making a lot of calls," Raleigh pointed out.

"It's a risk we'll have to deal with," Caroline interjected, fully aware that this was a necessary risk, one that was keeping their leader in balance. "Adrian, warn Charlie you'll be out of reach for a while; we don't know if our phones will still send and receive signals if we do this."

She pulled out her phone and sent a text, suddenly feeling an odd urge to lift up the curtain she had pulled down earlier in the day to see if the outsiders had any luck breaking down the front of the building. She figured, on the one hand, she might look out and see something terrible, but on the other hand, maybe the zombies had already wandered off.

Unable to control this strange urge, she lifted

up the curtain until she had about an inch's view of the outside world to find that all of the street lights and the sign in front of the building were still illuminated and (thankfully) not only had the zombies not gotten in, but they had lost the scent of whatever they were after and again were roaming around the streets. The streets, she couldn't help but notice, that were littered with the viscera of not only humans, but animals as well, with flies swarming around, and cars crashed into poles and each other, some just splattered with blood, undoubtedly from running down the zombies in the street.

Adrian could imagine the satisfaction of ramming your car into something that wanted to claw off your scalp and feed on your brain, taking your memories and your life. There was something to be said about killing in self defense: you can't just mow down a person who is getting on your nerves, but to do it in order to stay alive was a different thing.

Aside from how gruesome everything looked, nothing seemed different; traffic lights were still changing at what seemed to be the appropriate times, all the business signs seemed to still be on, and nothing looked to be out of power. It seemed right, given that the apocalypse hadn't been going on for long enough for any of the electricity to run out, but it was kind of a weird thing to see and think about.

Ch. 20
Anchorman

By the time Karl, Raleigh and Trevor were back in the room, Adrian took note that it was 1:35 AM. Although she had planned that they would get going soon, she wasn't ready mentally yet. She knew that in order to successfully accomplish anything, she and everybody else needed to have their heads straight; she hated in zombie stories when people did things impulsively, and she wasn't about to allow herself to be one of *those* people. In order to prepare herself, she pulled Raleigh aside and explained her hesitations.

"You... you're going to need some major counseling," Raleigh answered. "Here's what I want you to do: tell the others they can go back to sleep for a while, then you and I will find another safe room and talk there." Neither of them wanted a counseling session in front of others, but the idea of walking around a deserted building at night time had never been pleasing to Adrian. And doing it during the world's first zombie attack? Even worse. Multiple times when she was in for monitoring, she and her mom had gone on walks around the floor late at night and it had always creeped her out seeing all the lights off in the other rooms, when they had been bright and bursting with activity like crafting sessions and game night only hours prior.

"Do you think Karl's office would be safe?" Adrian wondered, knowing how close it was. "You were just there, how did it look?"

"We could go there," Raleigh mused. "I didn't suggest it because I noticed the tension between the two of you."

"That's definitely a thing, but if we *already* know it's safe..."

"Do you know whose offices you have next door?" she wondered. Adrian knew she had reporters on either side of her, but again, she'd never gotten around to knowing them well. She would sometimes hear the one to the left of her playing his music pretty loudly (what she would have done for that to be the case now) and rarely ever heard a sound from the one on the other side. She didn't know if either of them had been there this morning (they may have called in sick as well), but she hadn't seen them at the picnic, so either they were already infected, dead, or not in the building at all.

"I think we can use those rooms," Adrian decided. "I didn't see anyone there this morning."

"Tell everyone what's happening."

"Everyone!" Adrian announced. They all

immediately looked to her, wondering what could possibly be going on. "Hey, I have great news. First: who feels rested?" Absolutely no one said they did, so she went on, "I need to wrap a few things up before we go out. I'm going to the office next door for maybe an hour or so, so you can sleep a bit more if you'd like."

"Okay fuck you, Chase," Karl said, pointing an accusing finger. "I was sleeping fine, you had to wake me up and now you're saying I could have stayed asleep?"

"You're a dick," Adrian deadpanned, making sure everybody heard it. Addressing the room, Adrian went on, "Raleigh and I will be in one of the rooms next door if anything happens and you need one of us. And do us a favor? Don't need us." Knowing they were about to get more rest, they all agreed and wasted no time getting back to sleep.

Adrian cracked her door open and (seeing that the hallway was blessedly clear) signaled for Raleigh to follow her out. They went to the room directly to the left, but something was blocking the door from the inside. Either the employee had barricaded the room after realizing what was going on, or was dead and slumped against the door. Horrifyingly, both options seemed possible, the latter being more likely.

Moving on to the next room, the door opened with no trouble and was completely void of any living (or undead) beings. Adrian flicked the light on and entered the room, followed by Raleigh who slammed the door as loudly as she could. "We might have left a scent," Raleigh explained with a shrug. After sitting in the office chair behind the desk, Raleigh asked what was going on in Adrian's head.

"Tabitha!" Adrian blurted, much to the counselor's confusion. "This was Tabitha's office. She was *quiet*." She then went on, "Yeah, about your thing. I don't know but I've begun wondering what it's like to be infected. I mean face it: we wouldn't think it was such a bad thing anymore, we'd be safe (generally) and I just am worried because having thoughts like these could mean something's wrong with me." She thought about the things in a character's head in one of her books at the time they had realized they were infected. "I'm afraid I might give up with thoughts like this."

"Another Hank incident," Raleigh said, nodding. "What else can you tell me?"

Adrian did her best to articulate how her mind had come up with the simile of the zombies getting food versus how she felt about Charlie when she realized how badly she wanted to sleep with him, wondering why her brain had done that.

"If I'm right, you work in editing," Raleigh said, making a conscious effort to word it such that life would probably go back to normal any time now. "Am I correct?" Adrian nodded, so Raleigh went on to explain her theory. "I think this means that while you enjoy the news, you don't see things quite as black and white as those who write *for* the paper. You have a much more creative mind, which is what allowed you to come up with this comparison. And considering how often you read, you would naturally be wondering these things to want to know the accuracy of the books you like."

"What do I do if Charlie turns?" she went on. Raleigh wasn't quite ready for a sudden subject change, but Adrian was obviously in distress, so she offered up what she could. She started by asking if Adrian considered what they saw in the hall to have been Lucy, Nathan and the janitor. When Adrian admitted that, no, she didn't consider them to be those people any longer, Raleigh summarized that once you became infected, you were no longer you and therefore there was nothing wrong with being pushed out of everyone's life, whether that meant being killed or just never being seen again.

"You'd just move on and find someone else," Raleigh concluded, satisfied Adrian was through with the topic of Charlie. "Now I want to talk about Karl."

"Why?" Adrian said slightly more blatant than she would have liked. "It's not gonna do anything."

"I just think if we understood to at least some extent why he's being the way he's being, you'll be able to better manage it. I mean, not that calling him a dick isn't a way to manage it, but I mean a better way to manage it."

Adrian was hesitant, but pondered what Karl could *possibly* have against her; he was on the television constantly giving the weather report, whereas Adrian was in a position in the company that people never much thought about and maybe didn't even know existed, so it wasn't jealousy about her position...

Not convinced either of them would be able to figure it out through talking, Raleigh offered a service she liked to use in cases that felt a bit uncomfortable: she had incorporated tarot readings into her therapy sessions. Having gotten into psychology due to an interest in human nature, Raleigh decided to use these readings in session for people with an open mind, which definitely seemed to be the case with Adrian.

"It might help us decipher how to approach Karl," Raleigh explained. "If at all. The cards might tell us something that we should know that could make it a lot easier to get him to help out."

"That sounds interesting," Adrian said with a nod. "What would we have to do?" Raleigh explained the version of a reading she would do: a basic five card spread, which would tell something about the present, the past, and the future, with additionally showing reasons and causes. Finally, the fifth card can show possible outcomes, which in this case might be helpful in a lot of ways.

Adrian shuffled the deck of cards and set them out in the spread Raleigh had suggested.

Ch. 21
Frost/Nixon

"This is interesting," Raleigh said, examining the cards Adrian had set out. She had chosen The Fool, The Magician, Death, the Three of Cups, and the Ace of Wands. After a moment, Raleigh declared, "Wow, the cards are really telling it like it is today. See this card here?" She pointed at the Death card, which was the one about which Adrian had been most curious. "It seems bad, probably to you, but the death card doesn't necessarily only represent death itself. Like yeah, there are currently zombies roaming around the city, killing people and turning others, but since you placed it in this position, it more likely is trying to tell you that new beginnings are happening. It's calling you to accept the death of your life as Adrian, the News Sun editor who lived every day like an average citizen, and accept your new role as Adrian, the zombie fanatic who is helping a bunch of people from her office through the zombie apocalypse."

"So basically, this is it?" Adrain confirmed. "This is my life now and I just have to live with it?"

"Well yeah, but it's telling us that instead of thinking of this as a loss of normality, to consider it the start of something new and exciting. Also, it's pretty obvious that the rest of the reading is going to give us what we want, since the first card kind of sets the tone."

Raleigh took a look at the next card and stifled a laugh. "The Fool. This is fun; playing our role of the fool today is none other than Karl. Go ahead and put another card on this one to help me figure out what it's trying to tell us." Adrian shuffled through the deck and picked a card from the top half of the pile.

"Well that's pretty straightforward," Raleigh muttered, noting The Hanged Man had been set down. She adjusted her posture and gave Adrian the information she could tell from these two cards: Karl had his job because he's always considered himself an entertainer, so being stuck in the office all day with nobody paying any attention to him was really grating on his nerves. Although he always had a cocky attitude, at heart, Karl was much more vulnerable than he let on, as he hadn't gotten a great opportunity to socialize as a child, since people just didn't like him.

"It's basically saying that he needs to work on his own personal development, which unfortunately seems to involve getting along with you." Adrian was uncomfortable, thinking about being the vessel Karl used to figure out how to treat people, which Raleigh picked up on. "However," she jumped in, "since you then played The Hanged Man, this means further solidifies what I already expected. Karl does not have the knowledge in his head of how to work as a part of a team through just what he knows. He's not going to be able to cope until we're in a different situation, which could be never."

"Then what do we do?"

"The Hanged Man urges us to figure out who we are and where we fit in society. Karl has no idea of what that is for him now. Maybe you should suggest he give us a mini report on what's been going on today, what we know, and what we might do in the future. It'll put him back in the feeling of doing the thing he thinks he does best." Adrain nodded, thinking about how awkward it was for her to be in charge, not having ever started thinking about those normally in charge having to answer to her.

The next card Raleigh told her about was supposed to represent something about the future. The card in this position was The Magician, which Raleigh assumed was meant to be representative of Charlie, who was considered Adrian's "divine person", manifesting them coming together again, probably before too long. Adrian agreed that *maybe* that was what the card was representing, but she also knew that Nancy and Natalie had the same connection she did with Charlie, and asked if she could play a card of clarity to figure out who this card was meant for. She ended up playing The Devil as a card of clarity, which Raleigh explained could mean a few things.

"But if we're thinking The Magician isn't you and Charlie, then The Devil is telling us something else." She paused for a moment. "Actually, you know what? The Devil represents the realm of taboo; you and Charlie have been together for over 15 years. Nancy and Natalie only just got engaged. This is probably meant as them." After a bit of analysis, Adrian agreed that this was Nancy and Natalie, and further confirmed that she really needed to get the two of them together and in safety.

"What are these two?" Adrian asked, signaling to the two cards they hadn't talked about yet. Raleigh informed her that the Three of Cups represented teamwork. "It makes sense that one might come up for you. You've been pretty much forced to be the leader, but you're not exactly asking for help. That might be a cause of stress." The counselor had a good point.

Finally, Raleigh went on to explain The Ace of Wands and what it probably meant where it was placed.

"I can see you're really open minded to the idea of tarot," she began, given the amount of things the deck had already told them. "That's a good thing. I think this reading can really help you at least until we have our next move." The next move, Adrian already knew, which was getting them out of the building and to Nancy's fiancé.

"But what about when we do make our next move?" Adrian wondered. "Will we be safe?"

"That's the thing," Raleigh told her, "this Ace

of Wands is legitimately saying you're making a commitment to accomplish a task. The deck is suggesting that you're ready to spring into action, and that's good. You're not just blindly doing something, but you seem to be a leader and you're on the right path. But, maybe consider asking for help."
Adrian was silent for a moment.

"Huh," she said, "that's actually really helpful and interesting. I'm starting to feel more positive about what I've been and am planning on doing. Let's get back to the others and try to take the next steps."

With a nod, Raleigh went to check the hallway. She was dismayed to see an entire hall teeming with zombies, probably having picked up on the scent she and Adrian had left in the hallway. She motioned for her current companion who also saw the sheer mass of those outside.

"Wait it out?" Raleigh offered. As nice as that sounded, Adrian felt really motivated and did not want the adrenaline she felt to die out before she was able to make a next move. On top of that, if there were already that many zombies in the hall, there were undoubtedly more already on their way.

"We need to get back to our group," Adrian told her. "But we should talk more about the reading we just did. Loudly. We'll drive them away." Raleigh started expanding upon the Ace of Wands card, telling her that they could have drawn a clarity card for that, possibly to see if the next thing Adrian planned would work or if they should have made any changes. She got pretty in depth, talking about how

The Tower would probably be saying that whatever Adrian thought was a good plan would actually end rather poorly, but on the other side, were she to play The Moon, it would be urging her to do what she felt was right at her core being. The Moon was more about intuition and creativity, and Adrian wished she had played that card at some point.

The short walk back to Adrian's office was uneventful, although both Raleigh and Adrian were quite tense by the time they got back. A quick survey of the room showed that nobody had disappeared or turned, but they'd all decided to go back to sleep. Adrian and Raleigh began waking everyone up very gently to let them know what was happening next.

Ch. 22
Lions for Lambs

"Okay team," Adrian said addressing the room as a whole, "it's 2 in the morning. We're about to go out there. I don't want to be out any longer than completely necessary. I insist we make absolutely no stops. If we see anything that upsets us, no stopping to check and make sure it's actually true or try to prove anything else. If we freeze with fear, nobody is stopping to help us. We need to get it done, and we need it done *now*."

Having been in a cramped room for so many hours, nobody hesitated in lining up at the door with a partner, itching to get out into the hall.

"Before we go, I have a special request for Karl," Adrian said. He tensed up, expecting her to say something about being nice or not ranting about her, but was shocked when she went on, "Since Lucy isn't here, how about you give us a run down on everything that's happened today?"

"Can do," he said in his most authoritative tone. "Well, there are zombies in the hallway with a virus that begins as a person changing how they act. Shoot for the head is a good idea, and we're working on finding out more. Details tonight at eleven." He sang a little outro tune in his head, assuming everybody else did the same.

"You're all doing so great," Adrian said, using all of the motivation she could force herself to muster. "I'm really proud. We have to figure out how to get to the basement, passing as few people as possible." She stopped for a moment. "We'll have to pass certain areas no matter what route we take. Everybody okay on stairs? We can't trust the elevators right now. They can break, and... other things." She cringed inwardly, thinking about all the shows she'd seen in which an elevator chopped someone in half.

"We can only have to deal with two short staircases, if we're okay with a slightly longer walk down the first hall," Trevor suggested. Adrian looked at him suspiciously and he shrugged. "I try to avoid people, so I find routes to places."

"You come up front with me and lead," Adrian told him. "I don't know the route, and I trust you." With another shrug, Trevor walked to the front of the room and partnered with Adrian.

Taking a final (and possibly last) glance at the room she'd had as an office for the past twelve years, Adrian took a deep breath, opened the door, and stepped into the hallway. Everyone had been paired up, with Karl and Caroline bringing up the rear.

Adrian still didn't understand why and how they could endure each others' company: Karl'd been a jerk, Caroline a genuinely nice person.

Everyone launched into his or her own conversations about anything they could think of that wasn't zombies (Adrian was the only one who *truly* struggled with this) and started walking. Yelling would have probably made more sense than just a bunch of talking, but they'd all be more likely to lose their voices too soon if they spoke *too* loudly. It was close to 2:20 by now and they weren't incredibly sure how long they'd have in the dark if the mission *was* successful.

There was no way to ignore how creepy the atmosphere had become as they made their way into the hall and ventured to their final goal at that point in time: it was worse than earlier in the day when Adrian had been by herself because now she *knew* something was going on.

It didn't take long for her to realize that it would have been more helpful had she teamed up with Karl as fighting usually leads to yelling, which is loud. Karl and Caroline's voices did travel, however, although no one could tell what the two were talking about. Adrian truly wished she had Raleigh as a travel buddy, as she was feeling bad about Hank again.

At one point in their trip down the hall on the second floor they encountered zombie-Lucy which only served to make Adrian miss Hank that much more. She knew she was the group's leader, that Hank had spoken about how she knew everything that would be going on during a zombie apocalypse, but she was at the point no one really thought about: a main character or character extremely close to them absolutely losing it. She had assumed that that was Hank's position considering what he went through but apparently she was going to do it too. Thus, there in the middle of the hallway when she was completely aware of the fact that everyone with her needed her help more than she could possibly comprehend, she leaned against the wall, sliding down it and burying her face into her bent knees truly trying to disappear into the carpeting in this section of the hall. She effectively broke her own rule of not stopping for any reason.

"*What* are you doing?" Karl demanded, not helping the situation at all. Tear soaked eyes looked up at her group as Adrian admitted, "I give up. There is nothing any of us can possibly do to move on." The memory of Lucy changing at the picnic that afternoon was the only thing she could envision at the moment. "Who are we kidding; our only weapon is coins and they only weaken them. We thought they killed them, but Lucy was among the pack we thought we had killed earlier: they just stop them for a little bit. We don't even know that this mission is going to do anything." Her team had many theories about why she finally snapped, the most likely being that she hadn't talked to Charlie for a while. Also sleep deprivation: although she'd lived most of her life with that issue, this was obviously a different type as so many things were piled on top of it.

"Here's what I want you to do," Raleigh said,

sitting down next to her. "I want you to tell me the story of when you and your husband finally did that thing you were telling me about earlier. And remember: if you were able to get through that, you can get through this. There are people 100% behind you and not going to desert you."

"I'm not so sure about those two," Adrian deadpanned, pointing at Karl and Caroline, who seemed to have their minds on other things.

"Never mind them," Raleigh said. "Spare no details, but you have to walk with us as you tell me."

"Well," she said, standing up, "you see, what I did was replicate the first fancy date he and I had ever had."

"And what was that, exactly?" Adrian sighed.

"A horrible school Halloween dance that he legitimately asked me to the night of. We'd been dating since that Wednesday and I learned that he'd been crushing on me, but didn't have the guts to ask me out until the very last second."

"Were you in love? When you asked him to do this?"

Adrian laughed lightly and said, "We fell in love during the first date. He admitted it so I figured I'd have to be the one who proposed having sex." Her story consisted of when, where and how she admitted it, then the same about when they finally did the act (later that night when her college roommate was going to be at a party, then sleeping over at her boyfriend's).

She opened the door to the stairwell leading to floor one and continued talking. "We did it on the floor. My bunk was on the top and that didn't seem safe but our floor was nice. It was carpeted. And I'm positive it wasn't the first time the floor was used for that purpose."

By the time this story was over, they'd gotten to the door that lead to the front desk hallway, which was almost directly at the stairwell that went to the basement where the electricity was located.

As they turned the corner to the stairwell, the group froze in place, unable to force their feet to take another step. After a moment, Adrian realized why: Karen. She was sitting at her desk, even though technically she should have been off for the day, but she'd been viciously attacked. Every internal organ from her abdomen was laying in a heap next to her, falling from a gaping hole in her stomach. She sat motionless, her head turned upward looking at a ceiling it would never again see, her innards laying in a pile of blood and visceral goo.

"Was anyone close to her?" Adrian called out, wondering if anyone was going to be in a position similar to her after seeing this. The sight and stench was jolting. She realized that something within her had hoped that they would end up encountering living humans who they could get to join the team but it appeared that everyone was either a zombie or beyond dead. She got no response from anyone so they continued on their journey, all averting their eyes from the scene of this slaughter.

As they walked, discussing whatever odd topic they had chosen, nobody took note of the fact that they had entered into one off the tiled parts of the building until Nick slipped in a puddle of the cerebrospinal fluid left by the freshly infected. He landed on his arm in an awkward position, leaving it clearly sprained. The wail of the injured employee rang out far louder than anything earlier in the day, shocking everyone. Everybody stopped and surrounded the injured, helping him up, thankful that although he was clearly in a lot of pain, at least he could walk.

"I... I need a minute," he sighed, leaning on the wall. "This *really* hurts. I'm seeing stars." This was mostly directed at Denise who he was walking with, said in more of an apologetic tone than a pained one, as he continued explaining how he felt.

"I feel as if I've had a lot to drink. I'm dizzy, hallucinating and my hand feels like my head does when I'm hung over." With that, he proceeded to lean to the side and vomit an array of colors from the cheap lunch they'd gotten from the cafeteria. He then proceeded to continue vomiting stomach acid, as there was nothing left for his body to produce.

Now short of breath, he used his uninjured hand to push himself off the wall and cradle the injured one.

"I should warn you," he told Denise, "I'm not confident my body is done expelling things from itself."

"I mean, maybe Adrian will let us stop for ice," she told him, not at all hopeful that that would happen.

Everyone walked along until out of nowhere, Adrian blurted, "The kitchen!" All the employees (with the exception of the clearly angry injured Nick) looked at her, waiting for her to continue. "I'm thinking: we don't have much in the way of weapons, but the kitchen has some pretty sharp steak knives. I want to find out if there's something that keeps the zombies going; we can try cutting off certain parts of their bodies."

"Yeah that would be *great* if I could use my dominant hand," Nick said flatly.

"Can we also get him some ice?" Denise said hopefully.

"Great idea. We'll stop in the kitchen before shutting off the power so the ice stays frozen. Plus we'll actually have a chance of getting the zombies." Karl and Caroline liked this idea, since it would mean more special time alone for the two of them.

The kitchen was fairly close at this point, so they picked up the pace. He and Denise were forced to slow down, however, as walking faster made the injury feel even worse. He had to stop several times to vomit before they reached the kitchen. Denise did absolutely everything she could think of to help him through rubbing his back as they walked, as he got sick, and telling him stories throughout the entire trip.

By the time they reached the kitchen, a plan had been set into place. Everyone but Karl and Caroline would go in to compete the mission. Karl and Caroline were to keep watch, holding back any zombies that might pass by.

Instead of worrying too much about keeping watch, Caroline looked up at Karl, who stood nearly a foot taller than her. "I've been keeping my eye on you. Every night I'd catch you delivering the weather report and every day I'd hope to a higher power that you would get harassed by an employee and have to come to my office to talk about it."

"I am so fucking glad that you found our group before you got infected," Karl said, touching the side of her face.

"Thank goodness that you believed Adrian and joined the safety group. I have wanted to get with you for *so long,*" Caroline replied, stroking his nose seductively.

"This whole zombie attack thing isn't so bad, is it?" Karl said, half joking as he leaned in to kiss her again. They both knew nothing would ever have happened between them during work, as they worked several floors apart and nowhere close to each other's departments, they only got glimpses of each other in the halls when running errands or if they chose to break at the same time for lunch.

"Hey, if this works itself out, what do you say we go on a proper date?" Caroline brought her face close to his, replied, "Or even if it doesn't" and began kissing him once again.

180

Ch. 23
Control Room

If one were to ask the new couple if they'd had enough alone time while the other group got the knives and ice, the answer would have been a resounding no.

Nevertheless, they knew they had to go with the others to Adrian's office. But there were questions: did they get together out of desperation, or (a more hopeful option) were they actually into each other.

As they began their walk, they left Karl and Caroline in the back so they had to be very loud to be sure everyone heard their story, a story which consisted of Caroline having been watching Karl do the weather and not going on dates with anyone because typical first date stories usually are along the lines of family history and "why do you have that name?" (she made sure not to mention it), which would ultimately mean she wasn't free in case Karl ever approached her. Karl's story involved seeing a very attractive woman every now and then in the cafe but not knowing her name, where she worked, or her relationship status. He had assumed she was dating somebody considering how attractive she was, never guessing she was waiting for him.

"So yeah," Caroline concluded. "Now we're together." Not incredibly interested in their story, people began asking instead of the employee who slipped and how he was doing. Although they'd spent most of the day in a room with him, a few people still inquired about his name and position in the company because it didn't seem fair that he just be "the guy who slipped, hurt himself and began throwing up" but should be known by his name and job title.

"I'm Nick," he said. "I'm Nick and currently in intense pain. Why couldn't we have been stranded in a doctor's office instead of here?" The ice was serving less to numb his arm and more just an issue because it felt as if someone were dropping a hundred pound weight on his injury. "I work in Adrian's area, editing any mistakes in punctuation, spelling or the like. I am married but I'm not as close with my wife as Adrian and her husband clearly are... I mean, I called her to tell her what was happening, but—"

"Call her right now and tell her about your sprain," Raleigh interrupted. "One less phone as a flashlight isn't going to be a huge hassle and you clearly need to talk to her." He did his best to open his fossil of a flip phone that he refused to upgrade and dialed her number, one of the only ones he knew by heart.

As Nick made his call, Trevor mentioned that he would need help carrying the things he wanted to pick up. "Obviously we need the three radios I have, but I also have some fake weapons down there that could be helpful. Since Karl's staple gun thing didn't work."

"Didn't realize you needed to physically buy the staples for the gun," Karl said with a shrug.

"I know. But I have toy guns, which means we can shoot not only the darts it comes with, but also probably anything that would fit into the barrel. I suggest nails." Toy guns would never have occurred to Adrian, and once again she was thankful for the wide array of characters she had helping her. "I don't know if any of you know Morse code, but that would be the way to figure out if there's anybody out there with a radio," Trevor continued as they walked. "I know the basics like SOS, help, yes, and no. This form of communication was honestly created for situations not unlike this. If anyone picks up on the transmission, they can respond in Morse code."

Nick was just wrapping up his conversation when they finally reached the box that controlled all of the lights in the building, so two by two the group filed in, now in silence.

A casual glance at the room made it abundantly clear that it was Trevor's area: Nerf guns all along the wall with the darts stacked underneath them.

"Trevor, you work for IT, correct?" Denise asked. He nodded, so she went on, "Do you know how this box works?"

"Oh it's really quite simple," he replied, walking up to it. "Do those equipped have their flashlights on yet?" He watched as several employees held up phones already lit and a few more pushed buttons until their phones lit up. Nodding in satisfaction, Trevor went to the box and just flipped the switches to an off position. "This last one will turn off the lights down here," Trevor informed everybody. "But let's pick up the Nerf gear and the radios first." He instructed everyone on what to do: there was a motorized Nerf gun over on the left, but that one only worked with specific darts, and they didn't yet know if they'd be able to retrieve the darts after shooting the zombies, so that particular one could be rendered useless very quickly. There was another motorized one that could hold 50 darts, and he had a fair amount of spares, so he instructed Adrian and Karl to pick up that weapon and ammo from the wall.

Even though there were no zombies around right then, Adrian had to admit that she felt infinitely more powerful and competent simply by holding the toy gun she had in her hands. Now, geared with two things she had never imagined herself using, let alone in this scenario, she played with it to figure out how it worked. It was easy enough; apparently the only trick was that, much like an actual gun, this had a safety that needed to be cocked before a shot could be fired.

As Adrian inspected every element of this gun, Trevor went on with getting the other guns to other people. He picked up another of the weapons and laughed grimly. "Zombie Strike," he claimed, shaking his head. "Never thought this would be used in the actual situation." He'd originally picked it up for 60% off at a Black Friday sale, and kept it around the office at all times. Occasionally, he'd think about how funny it would be to randomly take it up to that one woman from the editing department and see how she reacted, but never that he'd give it to her to actually fight zombies. He had a few of these (they were a popular item among the IT crew), so he gave two of them to Denise, Karl, and Raleigh. Raleigh momentarily argued that she should not have a gun and should remain impartial, but was ultimately outvoted.

"The fun thing about these ones," he told them, "is that they don't require two hands to operate. If you cock it just using your thumb, it's easy enough to dual wield them." He glanced at Nick. "I mean, normally." Nick was looking particularly bad at this point, his face the same shade of green as the weapon. "But anyone who isn't carrying a gun, if you feel up to carrying some of the extra ammo, that'd be lovely." Nancy, Linda, and Nick went over to the wall and started picking up some of the extra packages that were there.

"What are these ones for?" Nancy asked, examining a container of what appeared to be miniature golf balls. Trevor hesitated. The fact was, he had an extra gun stocked a short way down the hall, and had been thinking about it this entire time, trying to figure out the best way to get to it.

"Um, another weapon," he told them. "It's not here, though. It's down the hall. We really need to get it, though, and also my radios are apparently in the room with it. If I could get one other person to come with me..."

"I'll do it," Nancy volunteered, as she thought Trevor was fun to be around, and she was getting a bit bored in the room.

"Cool. We'll leave the lights on for now, then turn them off once you and I get back." He loosely explained what they were going to do, then walked into the hallway. Nancy felt extremely jittery as they walked down the dank cement hallway, knowing that although there weren't that many rooms present, there could be zombies lurking anywhere.

"Say, how many people did you say worked in this department?" Nancy asked him, wondering how many of them had even shown up that day.

"Well, I'm department head, but I have five other guys working for me," he said, trying to calculate how much further they had to walk. They continued down the hall for a few minutes, Nancy taking note of the constant water dripping, and the random stains on the wall that were sure to be blood stains sooner than later. Finally, Trevor stopped suddenly and started pushing on the wall.

After a moment, a seemingly nonexistent doorway opened, and Nancy followed Trevor into the room. Laying in the middle of what looked to be an unused supply closet was a pink Nerf weapon, that Trevor explained used the golf ball-type ammo, and was his own personal weapon that nobody really knew he kept here.

"Oh no," he sighed, realizing he didn't have everything he thought. Glancing into the room, he saw his weapon, but only one radio. "Oh, they're gonna kill me."

He ran in, picked up the weapon then showed Nancy how it worked. It was the same as the other weapons in that you uncocked the safety and then it could fire, but it fired those small golf ball-type bullets.

"None of the guys liked trying to remember where this room was, so I used it for my own storage," he explained, picking the radio, which he traded Nancy for the gun. "I'm sure they all have stuff hidden somewhere around as well, but nobody liked anything about this closet, so it's mine."

"If I may ask, how the hell did you guys end up having all of these toy guns here at work?" Nancy wanted to know, trying to stop him from beating himself up about there only being one radio. "I can't imagine you just all showed up one day with Nerf weapons." It was actually a great story and Trevor had been hoping somebody would ask. A few Halloweens ago, Trevor had come dressed as a random army guy, complete with his Zombie Strike. Another of the people from IT had come as a police officer, and also had the same gun. During a lull in the day when nobody had any work to do, Trevor shot the guy with his weapon, and an all out battle took place. Over the next few days, random Nerf guns started showing up, and it became a thing among the downstairs crew that when they didn't have any work, they just had Nerf battles until they were assigned a task.

"The best part of it is, I mean you've seen what it's like down here," Trevor finished, "none of the higher ups had any idea. We could always get away with whatever we wanted, since nobody really ever wants to come down here." Nancy was well aware of what it was like at the office when there wasn't any work to do, but she usually would just either read or check news articles on her phone when she didn't have any tasks.

"So are we ready to go back, then?" Nancy asked now that all of that was cleared up. She wasn't looking forward to having all of the lights in the building turned off, so she was pushing to get back so it would just happen and she would try to convince herself that it wasn't actually as bad as she'd imagined. Trevor nodded, Nerf gun at the ready. He didn't expect to encounter any zombies on the way back, but it was nice to have the extra comfort of having a weapon in case they did.

Trevor pulled on the closet door, which swung open with much more ease than it had on the way in. Weather conditions had expanded it, so opening it meant it scraped against the floor and was fairly difficult to open on the way in. He and Nancy crept into the hallway, forgetting that they really should have been talking to one another, since the zombies seemed to be repelled by noise.

As the two quietly made their way back to the rest of the group, Nancy found herself lost in thought, considering all of the everyday things she'd taken for granted that she would probably never get to do again: video games, movie nights with Natalie, any form of medication, the list went on and on. Just as she was about to start ranking how terrible each thing would be, she was distracted by a moan coming from a short way down the hall.

"Now's your chance," she whispered to Trevor, reflexively being quiet so the zombie wouldn't notice them. Trevor pulled up his Nerf weapon and aimed it the way they do in the movies, slowly inching forward. Within a few seconds, the zombie's head jerked up, having noticed the smell of the two in the hallway. It seemed like it had been trying to find the bigger group, but here it had two victims who were trapped, and it actually knew where they were.

"Computer emergency?" Trevor asked, aiming the gun at the thing's head and firing. Time seemed to slow down as he watched it soar from the tip of his gun to the thing's head, planting itself firmly inside. The zombie fell backwards, probably still alive, but weakened. Trevor crept closer to inspect the damage, and saw green goo seeping out of its ears. It looked exactly like something from a cartoon, and probably would have been comical or entertaining, if he weren't standing directly next to the thing that could kill him. With a grimace, he bent down and plucked the ammo from the thing's forehead, releasing a huge burst of green gas that smelled similar to body odor.

"Smell ya later," Trevor told it, deciding that it was best to walk away now while it was still down instead of waiting to see if it reanimated. He'd gotten a hit of serotonin, seeing that thing go down with just a hit from a Nerf gun, and wanted to ride on that at least until they got back to Adrian's office.

"Why would this happen to us?" Nancy cried as they stepped over the zombie's body, still laying motionless in the middle of the hall. She was beginning to get really stressed out about all of the things she'd never do again, experiences she'd never be able to have now, and absolutely hated knowing that this was the world now. She'd given up all hope of a normal life, only holding on to the fact that Adrian had mentioned multiple times that she'd get to see Natalie again. She couldn't keep going if not for that.

"I don't know, dude," Trevor replied, shaking his head. "I don't know anything about any of this, either; I was always into the slasher films. I never even gave zombies any thought. But then, considering how much we've had to figure out for ourselves, I don't feel like Adrian's immense knowledge of the subject is turning out to be quite as helpful as we'd imagined."

"Just trying not to think about everything we'll never get to do again," Nancy admitted. "It's maddening, honestly. Like, don't sit down and think about it. We just need to focus on actually surviving. Never thought I'd get to this point in my life."

"It's a situation, to be sure," Trevor said, beginning to become annoyed with Nancy's prattling. They were in danger. They had been all day. How was she only just starting to get it?

Trying to push the annoyance from his mind, Trevor thought instead about what the best way to get back to Adrian's office would be once the lights were off. The trip was just a short walk down the hall, but he still felt really good about how the zombie went down, and oddly found himself hoping to encounter more to test the other weapons. Within a few short moments, Trevor and Nancy were back with the rest of the group. "Do you have any idea who that was in the hall?" Nancy finally asked, the question surprising both herself and him.

"It was Steve," Trevor replied, aloof. "Adrian has one of his Nerf weapons. Funny that that's what would do him in. But he was kind of an asshole, so I don't feel terrible about it." Addressing the entire group, he then asked, "Is everybody ready for me to turn off the power?" Without waiting for a response, he walked up to the fuse box. He stood for a moment, contemplating what was ultimately about to happen: he flipped this switch, and very probably, the power would never come on again in this building. Nobody was going to venture back downstairs to remedy the power outage, and in truth, this building would never be used again anyway. It would sit void of all humans, overrun by zombies.

Regardless, Trevor once again approached the fuse box, knowing that lights all around the building were already off. Finally, he flipped the one for the basement, leaving the group in total darkness. With a deep breath, he said, "That should do it. I guess those who have lights should be in the lead now?"

"If you don't have a light, try pairing with someone who does," Adrian said. "But I still want Denise and Nick together." After a few people chose a different person to walk with, the group (still lead by Adrian and ending with Karl and Caroline) found their way to the stairwell and began walking up it once again.

Although they all knew the condition Karen was still in, the lack of light worked to their advantage. They were unable to see too far ahead of themselves, and how to avoid lighting the area where her remains sat. The smell still hung in the air, piercing their nostrils so intensely that it stayed with them even after they were out of the smell zone.

As they climbed the first stairwell, Nancy brought something up. "Do any of us really know *anything* about each other?"

"Huh, I guess not," Adrian realized. "I guess it was just kind of, 'Do you have a craving for human flesh? No? Okay welcome to the crew. I don't know anything about any of your lives, and frankly I couldn't care less. It just like that we found each other and have banded together."

"It's nice," Denise agreed. "Whatever we did in our past no longer matters. If you ever reported something that was then found to be yellow journalism, no matter how bad you felt when it was discovered, now it doesn't matter. We're all friends now and have a fresh start."

"Exactly," Adrian went on. "I mean if any of you had addictions, none of us know so we're not about to try and change you. Unfortunately there's nothing we can do if you want alcohol or coffee or anything but we'll do what we can to help."

"We should definitely introduce ourselves once we get back," Raleigh insisted. "It'll be loud, anyway."

As this discussion transpired, Denise silently asked Nick how he was handling being on the stairs. He responded by shaking his head, wishing they didn't have to climb two stairwells that were so far apart. "Um, everyone," Denise called, "Nick's not doing well so we're going to stop for a while. The stairs are causing him a lot of pain and he's really pale." Since they had gone out in a group in case anything like this happened, they all stopped at the first landing the stairs offered.

"We should probably do something to help you," Adrian said, addressing Nick. "Personally, I'd call Charlie if I were injured, but I know you and the wife are going through a rough patch."

"I've got Denise now," Nick replied. "As long as she and I are always together, I'll be happy." He nudged her as he said this, once again displaying their office relationship.

"Not that we should be Karl and Caroline, but you probably want some type of physical comforting," Denise offered. "I'm here if you need it." Nick nodded, very happy that she was going to help and she went on, "Okay we need to make you a sling; supporting your arm with your other arm can't be doing much."

"I agree but what are we going to use?" Nick

said passively, almost annoyed.

"Until we figure that out, I'll handle it," Denise said. "Karl, give us your shirt."

"What the hell, Denise?" Karl asked, taking his white button down shirt off and passing it back. "You're the one who spends 24 hours at the gym." In truth, he did pretty much the same thing, having seen some weathermen (and women) who were very unenthusiastic and nearly got winded any time they tried to give the report in an upbeat manner that always just came off as bad acting.

As fast as she could, Denise wrapped the shirt around Nick's shoulder and tied it so that it made a sling to keep his arm steady. For a second, his injured arm tensed up when he laid it down, which did nothing but make it worse.

"It's okay," Denise told him. "We've got you. You can relax. Would more ice help?" They had retrieved an entire store bought bag which they planned to ration in order to get Nick through this injury.

"It's getting worse," he muttered, the pain in his wrist now shooting up his arm all the way to his shoulder.

"We need ice!" Denise called to Linda, who was standing around somewhere and had been assigned ice duty. She heard some shuffling and suddenly she saw Linda walking up to give her a small bag of ice. "Where do you need it?" she asked him.

"Literally at the point where my arm attaches to my hand," he said. She set it on his wrist, causing him to cringe. "Not. That," he said in pain through gritted teeth. Denise quickly snatched the ice off of his wrist, asking what was wrong. Panting, he said, "It hurts so much. It can't handle the weight." She returned the ice, this time not putting it down but keeping it on rather lightly. "Better?" she asked.

"Much," he replied, lucky to have the agreement they had. "I think I can walk now." They didn't need announce this to the group, they were all waiting nervously to find when they could keep going. Nobody bothered getting into their regular formation this time, just continued walking in a clump of people.

196

Ch. 24
The Hunting Party

"I just realized something," Linda said once they were on the second floor landing. "Sure Karen looked like shit and smelled like hell, but do we know that we're safe from her? Can she not pick up her internal organs, or just leave them there, and come searching for meat? Her brain hadn't been touched and isn't that the kind of thing you expect from a zombie: they get attacked but keep their brain then they attack?" Nick's arm throbbed suddenly, warning him that stress didn't help. He could perfectly envision her slowly sitting up from her chair, leaning down to pick up the organs she'd lost, or even yanking out what was left and coming to kill. He could imagine himself having a breakdown like Adrian just had.

Adrain didn't want to entertain the fact that the bodies she'd seen laying in the street not long ago shook off their injuries and were now also zombies. In much of the lore she'd consumed, being disemboweled did nothing to stop the zombies from hunting. In fact, even in the book she'd been reading that morning, disembowelment wasn't anything that would stop a zombie from roaming around.

Still trying to keep everyone going, however, she casually said, "Nah, I really don't think so. When I looked out the window at who had been attacked out there, they were completely dead. To become one of them you need a small bite, but being disemboweled means there's no coming back. Their sick minds get some kind of rush from killing but not fully devouring."

"I'm glad you're our leader," Nick said, his arm no longer throbbing from stress. Adrian felt bad about lying, but didn't want Nick any worse than he already was.

"Alright, who's ready to see what's going on in the hall?" Adrian asked, knowing that she herself wasn't ready. She could only picture how unprepared everyone else felt. Nobody spoke so Adrian reminded herself of the amount of pain Nick was in at the time and cracked the door and shone her small ray of light in order to peek into the hallway. A quick look showed that although was filled with zombies, it seemed safe since they weren't aware of the meat hiding behind the door. Reminding her of a dog who has heard the word "food" the zombies' demeanor immediately changed, as they perked up and began shuffling toward a door they could not see. Adrian wasted no time shutting the door and pinning her entire weight on it, inviting others to do the same in case they had gotten strong some time between when the group had left and now.

"What's going on?" Denise asked, worried about Nick.

"There are... *a lot* of them out there," Adrian struggled to say. "I'd say in the high thirties to low forties, and they smelled us. They know food is somewhere close by."

"So we just start being loud and they scatter," Denise said, her mind solely on taking care of Nick, rather than the group's immediate safety. "We can't just wait here until they leave now, can we?"

"Who's walking with Raleigh?" Adrian asked, her voice betraying the fact that she was on the verge of tears.

"That would be me," came Trevor's voice.

"We need to switch," Adrian said. There was a bit of shuffling as Nancy was replaced with Raleigh who started talking about what it's like working in the counseling department. Picking up on the plan, all of the other employees started talking to no one in particular about their jobs, and after a while, Adrian looked past the door once again. Although there were less of them by this point, those who were further down the hall weren't affected by the racket they were making. Still talking, she motioned for her group to join her and they trooped into the hall.

While they could have kept talking to scare off the zombies at the end of the hall, after discovering how Nerf weapons affected the zombies, now everyone was curious about whether or not the knives were a good idea.

"Everybody hush," Adrian said quietly. "If you have a knife, come to the front; I want to see if we can use them to kill." As Karl, Trevor and Linda joined her in the front, she added that anyone without a knife stay with Nick and Denise. There were six zombies in the hall: three employees, two of the children they had assumed escaped, and one person nobody could place. Linda had chosen the fact that a zombie could potentially fight back and therefore began by hacking off the arms of her pursuer, while Karl had chosen to simply chop off the zombie's head. To their extreme shock, neither of these techniques worked to stop the zombie attacks (even the headless one's body still had some juice in it), and suddenly the knives were just being slashed everywhere on the zombies' bodies. Trevor had the misfortune of being the one who had to attack the child zombies, and could not bring himself to do anything extreme to these young things, so had begun by punching one of them in the stomach to possibly slow it down.

On the other side of this was Adrian, who had officially blown her fuse and plunged the knife into her zombie's midsection, turned it to face upward, and pulled up, slicing through its stomach and neck, after which the knife cut open its head, the skull of which was nearly as easy to break as tissue paper. The dismembered body sank to the floor with no motion left whatsoever. She now understood the rush the zombies got by gutting their meals, although in her case it was for survival—along with taking out her anger at them for her friends' fates.

Noticing Karl, Linda and Trevor hadn't figured out that technique, she pushed them out of the way and replicated the action, these times pulling the knife out in a different direction to see if all worked. She shoved her knife into Karl's headless zombie's midsection and pulled the knife downward, causing the same effect: bringing it to a complete stop, the innards spilling out. Next she went for Linda's zombie, driving the knife into its body, but pulling it out on the right side. It stopped it as abruptly as the other two, but this one fell forward. Adrian jumped out of the way to avoid being covered with dead, graying organs.

All that this left was the two children, which Trevor had failed to get the courage to get rid of. He *had* been fairly successful in stunning them, however, as they made no move when Adrian positioned her weapon on the far left and pulled it across both of their midsections, cleanly splitting them both in two.

Panting and now filled with adrenaline, she turned to the other three and shook her head, chuckling at her counterparts' failures. The four of them returned to the other group and they continued walking, never looking back but wondering who they had just finished off. Considering how hacked up the four bodies had been left, they wouldn't have been able to have recognized the bodies of two children, their old lunch lady Chelsea, who had been decapitated by Karl, their old boss Nathan who was officially no more, sliced up with just Adrian's doing, the janitor who would never have to clean another mess, and a poor pizza delivery boy who was in the wrong place at the wrong time today. As much as she hated to admit it, Adrian had a feeling of sonder the entire time this was happening; she *knew* some of these people and was fully aware that they had had things to do: bright futures, important jobs, and probably families who had not yet gotten infected by the virus. She looked back at the mess in the hallway of the previously undead and now hacked up bodies, honestly feeling a sense of sorrow for those now absolutely never coming back, but forced herself to get over it upon remembering they had done the same and worse to her friend who could not control his emotions as well as the others in the company.

Ch. 25
Citizen Kane

Back at her office, Adrian was exhausted. They'd been going around all day, avoiding zombies, trying to figure everything out. It drains a person. Before she could collapse on the floor, however, she announced, "Okay, strictly speaking, I don't care what you do now. However, we should probably practice with the Nerf weapons. I'm sure Trevor can help us." Everybody except Nick thought playing with Nerf guns would be interesting, and a good way to take their minds off of the dangers in the hallway and outside, so started choosing what they wanted to use.

"Do you want me to stay?" Denise asked Nick, aware that he probably didn't want to be left alone. In truth, she also did not want to leave his side since through the years of their friendship, she admitted to herself that she had fallen for him, so she did not mind ignoring the Nerf thing to be with him.

In response, Nick snuggled up to her and put his head on her shoulder. It gave her a thrill that she hoped he didn't notice, and she agreed that she wouldn't leave his side. His pain wasn't going away with her presence, but she was a nice distraction.

Meanwhile, everyone Trevor had granted a Nerf weapon had gathered on the other side of the room to do some target practice. "We're going to start by shooting at large, stationary targets," he told everybody. "I want you to try hitting Adrian's desk." Trevor himself had gotten quite adept at shooting whatever he wanted, be it stationary or moving, so he wasn't practicing with the others. He did, however, revel in the fact that his expertise on toy guns was suddenly a skill that was sought after, and nobody was looking down on him for it.

Trevor watched as the darts flew, some hitting the desk, others flying straight past it. He hoped that those shooting were paying attention to where theirs went and why it missed the mark, as he'd allow those who hit the desk head on to continue to smaller targets, while the people who didn't do so well would have to continue practicing.

Once the shooting had stopped, Trevor told them what their next step would be: first and most important, go get the darts and reload your weapon. If you hit the desk, awesome, now go to the side and shoot at the smaller part of the desk. If not, continue practicing on the front instead of the side. Unsurprisingly, Raleigh was the only one who hadn't successfully hit the target.

Adrian, Karl and Nancy had no trouble with

the next challenge, so Trevor decided to kick it up a notch: he then instructed them to try hitting the trash can in the corner, which was only about three feet wide, as oppose to the five of Adrian's desk. Once Raleigh and the others had graduated from that task, it was time for some acting.

"I'm going to shuffle at you like a zombie would," Trevor told them. "I want you to try hitting me. Then we'll have others join the act." He stood on the other side of the room and started taking slow steps at them. It wasn't much of a challenge for them to hit him with the darts, so he sped up and started darting around a bit more. Maybe it's what the zombies would do.

While those five learned how to maneuver their weapons, Nick and Denise had time to bond a little more. Nick wasn't aware of the extent to which Denise was enjoying this, but had not ignored the fact that she'd wrapped her arm around him once he'd leaned his head on her shoulder. He hadn't shied away from what she was doing, and seemed to even be enjoying the extra comfort.

"So that sucks about your wife and you," Denise said, trying to keep Nick focused on something so he wouldn't fall asleep. Nick shrugged the shoulder of his good arm.

"It's whatever. I'm used to it by this point, but I can't ignore the fact that it took a goddamned zombie apocalypse to finally get her away from me." Suddenly, something came over Denise. This wasn't anywhere close to the type of thing she would have done in a normal circumstance, but high pressure situations get people into different modes than they'd usually behave.

"You like chaos," she observed, looking directly at him. "So you'd probably like it if I did this." With no hesitation whatsoever, she leaned in and kissed him with the passion she'd been holding in for over two years at this point.

"Do that again," Nick breathed after the fact. He'd developed some sort of feelings for her, although he couldn't quite pinpoint what they were until that exact moment: he and his wife were officially over, and he'd been ironically flirting with this woman for the past five years. This felt like the natural progression of things. They kissed again, and Nick fully gave into it: distracting him from the pain in his wrist, ignoring the horrors lurking just outside, and finally—*finally*—giving up on his emotionally abusive relationship with a wife who was long since over him.

"Office Wife," Nick said, "tell me something about yourself."

"Okay," she said. "Well I guess I've always liked helping people who were injured, so you're in good hands right now..."

"That's good," Nick said nodding. Then, holding up his injured arm, he joked, "I could really use a good hand." She rolled her eyes and went on to talk about what her life at home was like, why she liked helping injured people until Nick interrupted with, "I feel like this should be a whole group discussion. We're probably going to be here for a long time." Denise nodded and called out that they thought it was about time they started to get to know one another. All but Karl and Caroline gathered around those two, agreeing that it was a good idea.

"Wait," Adrian said before sitting down, "do any of you have wireless on your phone? I want to use the fact that they were avoiding the fish to try and figure out what caused this." Linda passed her phone to Adrian as they all sat to introduce themselves.

Adrian didn't pay a huge amount of attention as Denise continued to introduce herself, but instead searched "aversion to goldfish," only getting articles about food goldfish didn't like.

Changing up the wording, she then looked for "what don't like goldfish" only discovering information about how to properly take care of them. When she looked up "what goldfish eat besides fish food" she got a little more lucky. The article she found stated that they will eat meat, so she looked into what kind of meat they like. In an attempt to figure something out, while the page loaded, she returned to her board to write up what they knew. "infected were acting different, Nathan had an allergic reaction, he was late, they stay away from fish, fish eat meat" replaced the chart of employees they'd been making on her board. A forum she found with that search answered her question in ways that not only were unexpected, but thoroughly terrified her. Looking back and forth between the result and her scrawl of "*RASH*" written on the board in red, Adrian dropped the phone and screamed in a way that she would have called "unrealistic" were it in a film. Everyone in the room rushed over to her, now visibly trembling, wanting to know what happened. From her heap on the floor, she rose a shaking finger to look at the word that ultimately lead to the answer and what had been going on in the world.

Coaxing her out from under her desk with some deep breathing exercises, Raleigh asked Adrian to expand on the point of "rash."

"This morning, Nathan was late because he'd had an allergic reaction," Adrian stuttered. "He was hyper-allergic to mosquitoes, more so than most to the point that their bites had made him late several times. Hank had been talking to me about Lucy's arm which was almost entirely red because of several mosquito bites." Her speech was rapidly speeding up but those listening to her understood the point she was making.

Raleigh knelt down and put her hand on Adrian's shoulder in an attempt to comfort her. "How did you figure all of this out?"

"Goldfish," she managed to say. "And... the news. We and channel 9 were reporting the same bug report." At the mention this, Karl jumped in.

"She's right," he said. "One of the reports I would have been doing today was dealing with the fact that the population of the..." he paused, trying to remember if the bug was mosquitoes, or he was projecting the pronunciation of the insect "... mosquito were rapidly decreasing."

"What the fuck?" Trevor said, stringing the words together.

"It's mosquitoes," Karl returned as if that was common knowledge, not something Adrian had just figured out. "Something in the air must have mutated them so that after they bite someone, not only does that person have to deal with a terrible itch, but also a hunger for human flesh." Something tickled at the back of Linda's brain as she thought back to an animal biology class she'd taken in college.

"What do the goldfish have to do with it?" Nancy asked.

"They like the larvae of insects," Linda remembered.

"That would explain why the tanks didn't bother Lucy or Nathan," Adrian said, pumped up that they'd figured something out. "Those two had been infected for several hours."

"So we know the source of the infection, why they don't like what they don't like, but we don't know of their life spans," Trevor summarized. "Mosquitoes only live for, like a day, but what about when they're a hybrid mosquito/human?"

"I don't want to take anything for granted," Adrian said dismissively. "Let's just take what we know right now, kill any mosquitoes we see, and maybe come back to this later."

210

Ch. 26
The Constant Gardener

Upon realizing they might have a way to leave since they'd figured out such a vital detail, everyone wanted to get some rest. Nick and Denise went to the closest wall where they continued talking so Nick wouldn't be as focused on the pain in his wrist, Karl and Caroline returned to their spot to cuddle, and the others went to wherever they had space.

"Caroline, babe I'm really sorry but I *really* have to pee," Karl said, pushing away from their cuddle session.

"Do you want me to keep watch?" she asked, tracing circles on his chest, enjoying the opportunity to be open with him, but even more the fact that he didn't have a shirt on. Karl nodded absently, so the couple walked to the designated bathroom area that did not look much worse than when they had left earlier in the night.

As he was doing his business, Caroline started

laughing out of nowhere.

"What?" Karl asked, partially curious but more worried she was laughing at his piece.

"Oh I just think it's funny how most couples refuse to do this in front of each other for quite some time yet here we are: you've got it out, you're in the process of the act and... well, other things," Caroline replied. The "other things" of course were that if they *did* manage to kill off all of the infected beings and live in an uncontaminated zone, it would be up to the couples to repopulate.

Having finished what he needed to do, Karl made use of the stash of Purell Adrian had stumbled upon earlier in the day and returned to what now was his girlfriend, leading her back to the spot they had claimed as their own. His light blue eyes looked deep into her dark brown ones, clearly knowing what she meant by "other things" and said, "We *are* in a weird spot and as much as I'd like to do that, you're right: we've got to be responsible about it."

Adrian watched in horror by the low light the room provided as the couple once again began making out. She considered it possible that one of them may have been infected (not that she knew either of them very well, but this wasn't the read she'd gotten from them) or possibly worse, they actually were in love.

Nick and Denise took no notice of any of this going on, but instead continued to learn about one another, each becoming more intrigued by the others' life stories.

"Not that I don't find you absolutely

fascinating," Nick said once Denise had summed up her childhood, "but I feel like I need to call my actual wife again. You and I just kissed, which she'd end up finding out somehow if I don't tell her, and she might be able to help me figure out how to ignore the pain in my wrist. She was always pretty good at that kind of thing." Denise would have been offended that he was suddenly back to his wife, but had heard enough stories about her and how she reacted even any time he had to talk to a borderline attractive female for work, that she didn't bother making anything of it.

"Approximately how offended would you be if I got some sleep?" Denise returned, more trying to have something to do other than listen in on the conversation that was about to happen.

"Not even at all," he answered. With that, he got out his phone and promised to try to keep his voice down so as not to disturb her as she once again cuddled up against him. As it turned out, he didn't need to worry about his conversation waking her up, as his wife did not end up answering the phone. Several of the others in the room noticed him on the phone and gathered around.

"Well, she's dead," he said, his voice completely void of emotion. "She didn't answer."

Adrian suggested, "Maybe she didn't hear it, or her *phone* was dead, or—"

"She was totally OCD about her phone," Nick explained, shaking his head. "Always with her, on the highest volume, fully charged. I mean, she would have a panic attack if it got below 90%. And since she knows we're in a zombie apocalypse, she would have been sure to answer immediately."

"Shouldn't you be upset?" Karl inquired. Nick shrugged, admitting, "When I accepted what was going on, I emotionally detached myself from everything. I knew I ran the risk of never seeing her again, and honestly would only be upset if something happened to one of you. Mainly her." He gestured to the woman sleeping by his side.

"Well, we have to wake her up and tell her what happened," Caroline said. "Make sure she's okay, too." Caroline was actually incredibly stressed that someone was able to seemingly sleep so peacefully while all of this went on. Nick attributed it to the fact that Denise had been through a lot that day and must have wanted and needed a break from taking care of him. All of that being said, he agreed and gently nudged her shoulder. She wasted no time bolting up, wondering what had happened.

"We're all okay," Nick assured her, "it's just... my wife. My wife is dead. Or a zombie. Either way, it would seem she's out of the picture now but I feel nothing. It isn't a bother to me and they're all worried it's something to be concerned about." Denise looked at the couple of people who had convinced him to wake her up and nodded slowly. "I mean, I could care if I wanted to, but I don't. And I won't. Can we please just move on from this; hell, I'm more upset about my wrist than that this happened."

"Okay, everyone," Denise interjected, "obviously Nick is going through a lot here and not yet at the point where he wants to talk about it." Very discreetly, she shot him a look to let him know that she understood how he was (or rather wasn't) feeling. "Can we please all back off and let him figure his life out?" Truly wanting everyone to stay at their most mentally stable place, they all agreed and went back to what they had been doing before he had a breakdown.

Once they were all out of earshot, Denise asked, "So you're sure, right? You're not just putting on a brave face for all of us?"

"Please," he said, "after what I've seen today, I legitimately don't care that she's gone. As you know, our marriage was falling apart anyway; I was going to have to find someone else soon as it was. I'm pretty sure she was about to propose divorce."

Although everybody else had agreed to let Nick work through this on his own, the counselor could never stop herself when she heard somebody say the word "propose" or "divorce", not to mention both words in a row.

"Nick," Raleigh said, joining him and Denise on the floor, "you definitely seem to be experiencing a sense of something called *mauerbauertraurigkeit.*"

"I'm going to *pretend* I have any idea what that word means and agree with you," he said.

"Sorry," she admitted, "counselor, German minor, sometimes forget that's a word people don't know." Germans had a word for everything. "What I'm saying is you seem to be trying to push us all away. Sure you're willing to talk to Denise, but she's letting you ignore how you might be feeling about what just happened."

"Here's the thing," Nick said in return, "I'm going to explain what's been going on in my life and why I really don't care, but honestly, y'all probably cared about anyone who might have died." As he told her how he was feeling about their situation, she could tell he was giving spare details because he didn't believe anybody would be able to relate to what was happening for him. This, paired with the fact that it was obvious that he wanted to not care about the few things that still mattered to him (mainly the fact that he'd been injured) and the only thing he thought he had in common with everyone else was that they wanted to stay alive, concerned Raleigh.

"Sorry to dump this all on you," he said once he'd explained his point of view. "I'm sure you have better things to worry about."

"I'm a trained professional," she reminded him. "I'll leave you and Denise alone. I feel that your talking about this is going to help you in the long run, though. We all need to do what we can."

"This is true."

And she left, leaving Nick now alone to speak with Denise.

"*Is* all of that true?" she asked him. "That story about your wife?" He nodded his head. Denise took a moment to consider the golden opportunity she now had in front of her: Nick was emotionally dead, so not grieving his wife. There wasn't any feeling there at the moment. She needed to say something before this sunk in.

"So, by all accounts, you're single now, right?" Denise made sure. "So, the fact that you and I were just kissing was... she'll never find out." Nick shook his head in confirmation. "Okay, cool." She hesitated. This felt like a perfect time to admit her feelings to him, but worried it might be some form of harassment. But no, she just wanted to tell him while he was in the semi-positive mindset.

"What's going on?" Nick asked her, noticing how uncomfortable she had suddenly become. Denise relayed it all to him: that time she had an anxiety attack and passed out right before the two of them were going to go for an after work coffee? That's when Denise had realized she was in love with him. But of course he could never know this, as he was a married man and although they were friends, she wasn't going to overstep any boundaries. Now that he was... less of a married man, she felt like it was alright to let him know this tiny detail.

Nick allowed himself a few moments to process what Denise had just unloaded, considering how much of a toll it had clearly been taking on her these past few years. Without any hesitation, he admitted that he felt the same way about her, even though he hadn't ever actually put words to it.

Denise couldn't exactly understand his ability to admit that so quickly after losing his wife, considering how much emotional damage that should have put him through, but at the same time, she herself had done a pretty good job of detaching herself from everything in her life. In a sense, really all that mattered from here on out would be surviving, so past life wouldn't really need to be involved.

"So, we're a couple now? Official?" Denise asked.

"I mean, we're in love and both single as of today, so it makes sense. Plus, you're not a manipulative bitch like my wife was."

"None of this is normal," Denise said. "And I don't just mean the fact that there are flesh eating monsters out there right now. That being said, okay yeah we can be together now."

Although he would have never admitted it out loud, the thought crossed Nick's mind that there was a chance the strong emotions they were feeling at that point were just because they wanted to feel *something* good. Thinking about how he'd felt when she came to help him in the stairwell, taken her time walking with him to the kitchen, and honestly caring about him through this entire ordeal made him realize that no it wasn't just an "in the moment" thing; there was definitely something there.

Realizing what was going on between the two of them, Adrian's emotional stability was pushed further toward its boundaries. She understood how people in dire situations acted in ways they normally never would, but what was going on between those two seemed genuine. She longed to be able to do something similar, but she knew (*hoped!*) she still had Charlie waiting for her at home. There was nothing she could do about that aside from know that he had taken her for her word and was in the basement away from everything that was happening and would more than likely be alright in the end. She hated that he had the sickness he had and wished she could do something to help him, but knew he had medicine if he absolutely needed it. As bad as they were, his migraines had never lasted for longer than 24 hours.

220

Ch. 27
The Insider

The possibility never occurred to Adrian Chase that miles away, in a small house usually accompanied by both Charlie Baker *and* her, a plan was being set into action.

Finally fed up with being stuck in the dingy basement of the tiny, inexpensive house they had bought after pooling the money they had left after their wedding, he had decided enough was enough and that he was going to go save his wife. After three years of being married, he couldn't just leave her in a zombie infested building when their house had boarded up doors and windows (a safety protocol he had taken directly after she told him what was going on in the world) where she and the others would be completely safe.

'They hate noise,' he thought to himself. 'Noise...'

Adrian's entire party was still wide awake even with the low light, late time and exhaustion of the day. The tap on the window startled them and they immediately rushed to it, wondering if the zombies had learned to climb. It had come to the employees' attention that the zombies became able to adapt to their situation the longer they were infected: at some point they seemed to stop avoiding the fish tanks and they required more food to function, among other things.

The sound outside was not a constant tapping like that of a zombie's finger, but only occurred every few moments, rarely at the same volume.

Adrian knew she was technically the leader, so even though she didn't think there was anything horrible out there, she preferred nobody else saw what she'd seen earlier. Pushing everyone away, she decided to open the curtain to see what was making the noise. As she approached the window, she heard the muffled sound of some music playing, along with the occasional knocks. After a brief moment she knew exactly what it was: Charlie was blaring a song about Star Trek by a band called Five Year Mission that lived about two hours away from them.

She pulled up the blinds and there stood Charlie Baker holding his new speakers above his head, like a teenaged boy trying to prove his love for the girl who had just broken up with him, blaring a playlist of Adrian's favorite tracks. Around him lurked absolutely no zombies, as this early morning music presentation was loud enough to keep them at least twenty feet away in every direction. It appeared that he brought a car, almost out of view in the office's parking lot.

"Who's that?" Nick asked, everyone now behind Adrian and also looking out the window. Totally defeated Adrian's attempt to not allow them to see how terrible it looked outside.

"That's Charlie!" she said. "Guys, Charlie braved the zombies and came out to save us! We have to go downstairs, unlock the doors and let him know what we know!"

"He seems to know the noise thing, anyway," Nick muttered.

"But he doesn't know about what *causes* it!" Adrian realized, as she hadn't spoken with him since they'd figured this out.

She opened the window to her office. She waved her hand downward rapidly so he would turn down the music and she could warn him.

"Get back to your car!" she called. "It's caused by mosquito bites!"

Charlie's face dropped, a look of absolute terror taking over the smug look of having figured out how to keep the zombies away, making it clear that no he *hadn't* figured that part out. He turned the music back on, set the box down, and ran back to his car.

Adrian turned back to the group and said, "We're going to go out there. Charlie wouldn't risk his life for me without having a plan, and.... well we're obviously getting nowhere trying to figure out what to do. He left the box playing, and as long as we keep the volume up in here, we can make it out to the box and the car without any trouble."

"Yeah he would," Karl said sarcastically. "Also, you *do* realize there are still those things in the hallway, right?"

Adrian couldn't contain her frustration at him anymore. "Why don't you just go over to your girlfriend and talk about why you hate me while we go downstairs and out to see Charlie." She paused. "Before I hit you. Come on guys, this is probably the best thing that's happened to us all day." She didn't want to discount Caroline's appearance, but she knew she wasn't functioning that well without her husband. "We can't just ignore the fact that there is a person down there who can possibly get us to safety."

"She's right," Raleigh piped up. "We all have to go. I'll walk with Adrian, and I want Caroline to walk with Karl, Nick with Denise, and Trevor with Linda." She said this last part as a side thought, as the two of them were only paired with each other because the other matches felt connections with each other. Still, it was a relief that they happened to pair each with a friend for travel. They tried to ignore the fact that the group used to be bigger.

"I really don't want to do this," Adrian whined, all too aware that this was her order in the first place. She would have been completely fine with waiting out their days in her office were it not for her husband. He was known for keeping his head together in crisis, and she *really* needed that after the day she'd had.

"It's going to be okay, we're going to be okay,

he'll be fine," Raleigh said, noticing that Adrian she was being uncharacteristically quiet.

"I mean, I *know* that, but I'm still scared," Adrian explained. "Everything hurts and nothing is good."

"We all think that, but we'll see what happens when we get downstairs," Raleigh told her. In a flash, Adrian realized that Raleigh was distracting her, and they were already in the hallway leading toward the stairs being fairly loud as they walked.

"I'm just nervous," Adrian explained. "On top of the fact that we're living through the zombie apocalypse, I'm the leader and Hank is gone, I don't know how long Charlie was out of the basement preparing to come and get us. Plus I don't know which car he drove; he drives a five seater and I drive a four. I'm actually really scared." She didn't doubt that the stress would make her start throwing up soon, so she blurted, "Everyone look out for puddles, we don't want another Nick incident."

"Jerk," he called from the end of the (admittedly short) line.

"Hey I'm just saying," she replied with a shrug. Then for Raleigh's ears only, she said, "But in all fairness I think I might be sick."

"Just get to Charlie and we'll see how you're doing," Raleigh told her, rubbing her back to help her calm down. "We know he's alive and alright—"

"Do we though?" Adrian demanded, once again feeling herself being pushed to the edge. "I told him to stay in his corner in the basement, and yet here he is, completely ignoring my advice, something he wouldn't normally do. We know absolutely *nothing*."

Raleigh turned around and made everyone stop for a short break. They all looked at her, puzzled and a little annoyed.

"Adrian isn't doing so well," she explained. "If you're doing okay, keep watch for any of them while she calms down a little bit." Once again, Adrian had elected to sit on the floor to gather herself, completely ignoring how macabre the carpet onto which she had sank had become. Raleigh forced herself to sit as well as they waited for Adrian to calm down.

"Remember earlier when you told me about your first time getting with Charlie?" she told the employee who was now huddled up, trying to ignore everything that had happened and that was going to happen in the days, weeks, months and years to come. Adrian nodded, wondering where she could *possibly* be going with this. "If I'm correct, your wedding was only a few years ago."

"It was," Adrian said, visibly perking up as she knew she was going to be asked to describe it.

"You can tell me about it, but only if you start feel better and walking," Raleigh told her.

Adrian realized that this was the obvious thing for Raleigh to say, but she did manage to get herself together and stand up. She began by talking about the dress that she had picked out, exactly the kind that was common at weddings, along with Charlie's tuxedo, very nice but still not particularly interesting. Regardless of these facts, she and her soon to be husband felt very special standing at the front of the church, knowing they were about to officially be husband and wife and then move into an actual house with each other.

"And we've never regretted that decision," she said wistfully.

228

Ch. 28
Deadline USA

"See, that wasn't so difficult, was it?" Raleigh said.

Adrian realized where they were: down the hall, down the stairs and about to enter into the lobby where they had found Karen's remains earlier in the night.

"Everything smells so bad, though," Adrian argued, realizing she'd had her mouth open for much of the trip. She realized that they didn't know much about the virus and could only hope that the air around them wasn't swarming with germs, just waiting for some stupid human who didn't realize that they could inject themselves into the throats and turn them into one of the monsters that were all around them.

"You were doing fine a minute ago," Raleigh observed. "What's going on with you right now?"

Adrian explained the completely unwelcome

thought that was swimming in her head at the time. She was also anxious because they either were or were not about to see Karen, completely dismembered, still at her desk, having been doing exactly what she was meant to, or an empty desk where she had been.

"We should have warned her," Adrian wailed. Although making sure Karen was okay obviously was never a part of the plan since the zombies already had gotten to her, Adrian couldn't help mourning all of the lives they had lost that day.

She needed something to distract herself from what they might be encountering in just a few short minutes so she called, "Okay everyone, I know that technically we all know each other by now, but one by one I want us to say our names, relationship status and job in the company. I'll start: my name is Adrian Chase, I'm married to the man who came to save us, and I worked in Fact Checking."

"My name's Raleigh Shapiro, I'm single, and I was the therapist for those who needed it—and may I add, there really weren't many of them." Adrian had always wondered whether or not Hank had talked to the therapist about how he had to completely change his life from what he had planned on doing in the business compared to where he ended up. She knew that Raleigh couldn't talk about people who went to see her, so even if she acknowledged that Hank was one of her patients, she couldn't say what they talked about. Adrian wasn't going to go up to Hank and say, "Is your life so screwed up that you talk to the company's therapist?"

"Was Hank one of the ones who came to see you?" Adrian blurted without realizing what she was doing. Apparently it had been bothering her more than she gave it credit for.

"We're not really supposed to—"

"*Pretty sure* he's not going to care if you say it," Adrian said, going out of her way to sound rude.

"Um, Karl what are you in the company?" Raleigh said in a panic. She then whispered to Adrian, "I'll talk to you later."

"I'm Karl Aster, dating Caroline (if you hadn't picked up on that yet), and I was mostly the weather guy, but Nathan regularly asked me to fill in as Head Reporter (yeah, be jealous), which is how I knew about the fucking bugs screwing everything up. Fuck them. Seriously."

"Let it all out," Caroline told him, rubbing his back. "Anyway, my name isn't actually Caroline, but you don't need to know about that, and my last name is Fiala. I just worked in the HR department, unfortunately keeping me away from *this one,* which I'm so glad we were able to fix this evening."

"You... you went out of order," Nick mumbled, still drowsy with pain. He needed another reason to be upset. The pain was getting to be unbearable.

"I love you," Denise whispered, realizing how poorly he was doing. Nick smiled, thinking back on all the time they'd spent together through the years of their friendship and the time they'd undoubtedly be spending together now. He had a special talent for reading people, and he could tell how deeply and truly she meant what she said.

Even though he was glad to have Denise as a girlfriend now, he was in pain and couldn't help wondering if anyone would be worse off were he to give himself up like Hank did. He knew there was nothing anyone could do about what had happened to him, but on top of being in immeasurable pain, he felt beyond stupid for having not noticed the puddle he had slipped in.

"Why don't you go next," Linda said, understanding exactly what was going through his head. "And it's not your fault, your walking buddy should have been looking out for you."

"Oh my God, shut *up!*" Denise shouted, absolutely enraged. "Nobody else in the party saw the puddles on the floor, anyone was allowed to warn anyone about that danger!"

"Okay but you all pretty much know me," Nick replied, ignoring the accusation she had shot toward Denise. "Nick Nicholas (don't ask), my wife is done for but was going to divorce me anyway, so now I'm with Denise who is lovely. As I mentioned earlier I used to work in Adrian's department as a punctuation and spelling expert. I'm probably the coolest person you'll ever meet."

"So, hi everyone, I'm Denise Jenkins and apparently the reason Nick here hurt himself, but now I'm dating him and I worked in sports and occasionally a fill-in reporter," Denise said. "Any time Karl, Nancy or Lucy were all out sick or had something come up, I'd have to come in and do their report for them."

"Sorry about those times," Nancy said,

deciding it would be good for her to go next. "I'm Nancy Gaspirtz, I'm in a relationship, and I was an intern who filled in sometimes."

As always, Adrian worried about how Hank was after hearing that. Then she remembered what happened.

"God dammit," Adrian muttered.

"You alright there, Adrian?" Raleigh asked.

Adrian chose not to say anything because she knew there would be no way to describe the ongoing pain she felt at anything that had the tiniest relation to her friend Hank. She didn't know how to explain that Hank dying made everything else feel less important. That was why she had really clung on to the thought of Charlie still being around; but now that he was and he was saving them, it still didn't make losing Hank any less important. She waved it off and urged Nancy to continue with her introduction, even though they all knew her relationship status.

By the time Nancy had finished introducing herself, they had reached the door leading to the lobby where Karen's body may or may not have been located. After seeing all the corpses the zombies had left disemboweled, Adrian had almost no doubt that the body would still be there; after all, as she'd found out with Hank, it didn't seem like they liked to hold back when they were enjoying whatever they currently had at their fingers.

"Are we all as ready as we'll ever be?" Adrian asked, knowing all she was doing was a stall. The team nodded. She took a deep breath, squeezed her eyes shut and pushed on the door with the entire right side of her body. The stench that immediately washed over them was not the one they'd been expecting. Instead of the smell of dead body, the smell was that of zombie, which was a completely different category: it included that of human waste, rot, and blood.

Trevor pushed to the front, Nerf gun at the ready, reasoning that Karen had come back. True enough, what they had assumed was a corpse had come back and was standing in the corner of the room, her guts trailing behind her as Adrian had not expected at all. There were even bits of it that had rotted off, strewn across the carpet.

The second Trevor's smell hit what Karen had become, the zombie slowly turned around, her abdomen covered in her own blackened blood.

"The black blood *is* the zombie blood," Adrian observed, always wondering if it was zombie blood or really old human blood displayed on the undead.

Trevor started shooting at Karen, a Nerf weapon in both hands. His aim wasn't as good as he'd convinced himself it would be, and of the ten darts he shot, three of them hit her: one in the arm, one in the neck, and one in her shoulder. All three darts sunk into her body, and she did fall to the ground. She was still twitching, however, as none of them nailed her in the head.

As the body wasn't completely done for, Karl went up to it, hoping to prove that he would do whatever he needed to protect Caroline. He was holding one of the Nerf weapons that had the golf ball type darts, and stood within a two foot range of Karen. He aimed and shot two times, both darts hitting hard and sinking in as he'd hoped.

He retrieved all of the expended ammo before the smell got too bad to handle, and returned to the group, handing Trevor's darts back to him.

"So that answers that," Adrian said with a sigh.

Now that Karen was officially dead, they felt completely safe in this one room, even safer than when they'd been holed up in Adrian's office. Nobody said anything as they made their way across the room, savoring the temporary feeling, but not being particularly comfortable in the same area as Karen's work station.

Although there were no clear signs that any more of the undead might be anywhere nearby, everyone remained cautious. The room they were making their way across was fairly large and there were doors on every wall leading to the different floors and separate rooms around them.

"So the security on the door is turned off, right?" Adrian asked Trevor.

"Shouldn't be an issue," Trevor replied. "As a safety feature, the lock you guys took care of this morning is shut off when the power goes out in case those still in the building would need to get out."

"Wonderful." They had made their way to the door by this point, forcing them to stop and see what lay ahead.

Ch. 29
A Mighty Heart

A group of zombies stood at the door in various stares of decay. By far the most cadaverous of the bunch was Lucy, and one couldn't help but wonder if she was the first not only at News Sun, but maybe even in the world. It was odd, jolting even, to see this petite woman in such a state: her skin, which in life, only hours ago, had gone from a light caramel brown to a stark grey accented with marbled green, her hair a tangled mess of what had to be the blood and brains that didn't quite make it to her mouth. Among the many faces, it was also easy to identify George, the day janitor who worked Mondays, Wednesdays, and Fridays from 9 AM until 3 PM.

Looking at all the zombies and recognizing nearly every one of them, each survivor had questions. Ignoring the danger facing them, Karl was curious if they had turned mostly from getting bitten, or if it was because of the mosquito bites. As a therapist, Raleigh wondered if the zombies were conscious of what they were doing, and if so, how did it make them feel emotionally. Nick, now numb to most emotions himself, only wanted to know why each one looked the way they did: as Lucy seemed to be the only one with mass amounts of gore clinging to her, why was it? Was there still some cogent thought, a spark of being a vegan left in her that knew it was doing something wrong, was it just because she had suddenly become clumsy, or (far most likely) did she just enjoy playing with her food.

As more of an outsider to the company, Trevor did not recognize these people aside from knowing he'd passed them in the hall at times. He was stuck with a thought that was going to sink in with all of them in time: at some point, on this day, each and every one of these now zombies had been somewhere in the building, dead. And, if Adrian's account of what had happened was true, they weren't even stone-cold dead. After seeing Lucy at the picnic, obviously her blood was still warm when she turned, but now Adrian knew this wasn't always the case. Now people were dying and then coming back.

And Adrian, the "enthusiast" of the group, had a morbid curiosity of whether or not they *were* all, in fact, mindless zombies, or did they remember the group standing in front of them as coworkers of a time passed.

Before Adrian had the chance to tell anyone what to do, Nerf darts were flying through the air towards the zombies. One hit Lucy square in the eye, the force of it causing her eyeball to explode. She staggered backwards, black goo now leaking from her eye socket, then suddenly found her footing and lunged forward. Adrian ducked as the zombie clumsily punched at her and Linda drove one of the knives into Lucy's neck. Her instincts suddenly kicking in, Linda next twisted the knife so it was facing outwards, and chopped Lucy's head almost clean off.

"This is what being a pretentious vegan does to you," Linda spat as Lucy's corpse hit the floor.

Adrian felt very uncomfortable, both knowing the zombie that had just been annihilated, and having known Hank's feelings for her. There was something incredibly satisfying about their own Patient Zero being finished off, but she wouldn't have wanted it to be Lucy.

As Adrian had these thoughts, she realized that without paying any attention to them, the other zombies had scattered in other directions, as the humans didn't seem scared of them anymore. Since the path was clear, she completely broke the pre-established protocol of staying with your walking buddy, and rushed past the boom box that was still blaring its loud music, and ran to Charlie. To her horror, he was sitting in in the front seat of the stereotypical 80s love-mobile they kept hidden in their garage.

Seeing the look on Adrian's face, Charlie immediately explained his reasoning. "I noticed how few zombie-cliches you'd lived through today and I just felt like an old, scary van would be the most cliché thing we could drive. And anyway, your Ford wouldn't hold more than about four people and I knew you had a group." He had a point, but Adrian was still slightly upset that he had chosen this vehicle. Until she opened the door and discovered what was inside the van: he had brought along cases of bottled water, an entire store of boxed cereal and bags of chips, enough food for them all to live on until they got this all figured out. He had also thought to bring along blow up mattresses, blankets, pillows, everything one would bring if they were doing something as simple as going camping, but, in this case, possibly life-saving.

"I have never loved you more," Adrian told him, still staring at everything he had brought.

"There's more," he told her.

"Stop talking," Adrian demanded, immediately giving him a kiss that she had spent the whole day wondering if she would ever be able to give him again. In that kiss, everything melted around them: it no longer struck her that it was four in the morning during the world's first ever zombie apocalypse. All that mattered was Charlie: his lips pressed against hers, and the feeling of togetherness that she had worried all day she would never experience again.

The two of them were so distracted, that neither noticed the rest of the team had gotten into the van and the boombox had been turned off until a quite rude "Ahem" came from the back seat.

"I'm gonna assume that one's Karl," Charlie said, separating himself from his wife. Adrian nodded as the motor roared to life.

"As I was saying," Charlie said, "do you think anyone else knows it's mosquitoes?"

"No," Adrian replied.

"Good."

As they drove, those who were yet to introduce themselves gave their speeches: they found that Trevor's last name was Walsh (they all knew he was an IT guy who wasn't dating anyone), Linda's Monette (she arranged the articles in the paper once they'd been written). Adrian realized that they were heading to the local convenience store and panicked.

"What are you doing?" she gasped, managing to be heard over the sound of the engine. "It's going to be crawling with them!"

With a grin, Charlie said, "Well I figured you probably had a lot of adrenaline to use up, and in this brilliant world of technology, there is actually an invention that drives bugs away." She thought about how it felt in the hallway when she took care of those attacking her and her friends and completely understood where Charlie was coming from: the two of them would enter the store, she would take care of anyone who attacked them, and he would stock up on as much bug spray as he could carry.

"Grab some rye flour and baking soda, if you will," Denise blurted all of a sudden.

"Wait, why?" Adrian wondered. It wasn't like they'd be cooking anything.

"So, you remember how Lucy was a vegan? Nick and I are eco friendly, and—"

"I'll do it if you shut up," came Adrian's reply.

She thought about how it felt in the hallway when she took got rid of the group of zombies that Karl, Linda and Trevor hadn't managed to take care of, and completely understood where Charlie was coming from: the two of them would enter the store, she would take care of anyone who attacked them, and he would stock up on as much repellent as he could carry.

Adrian braced herself as they pulled into the store's parking lot. It looked like it belonged in one of her books: the glass was cracked and covered in zombie guts. It had clearly been broken into earlier as people looked for supplies.

She grabbed two of the knives they'd brought with them, told the others to stay in the van, turned the music back on full blast (hoping nobody would complain about the music's content), and opened the door. She and Charlie met at the front of the van, joined hands and walked in silence to the still functioning automated front door of the building.

Neither of them said anything as they did this, their silence almost taunting the zombies to come attack them. Within seconds, there was movement in the shadows. It would have set Adrian on edge in a normal circumstance, but it turned these two into the machines they needed to be, separating the thought of these being people (which they weren't) from their need to stay alive, and having no trouble doing exactly what they needed to do to. There really wasn't much difference between these things and human cadavers that medical students operated on.

In much the same way as highway hypnosis,

Adrian's mind became something that instead of consciously knowing what it was doing, simply forced her to do the job her body needed to do; stabbing the zombies and making sure they went down, hard.

Mere minutes after the first attack, Adrian and Charlie found themselves standing back to back, panting, and surrounded by bodies of what used to be zombies, now with gruesome, thick puddles of black goo, the odd arms and legs scattered about. The two of them stood, trying to figure out their next move, finally stepping over what was surrounding them and walking into the building.

Charlie was not expecting the automatic door to so easily slide open as they approached, as everything around them was so dead. He and Adrian gingerly stepped inside, only to be greeted with a reminder of what the world had gone to within less than 24 hours: shelves emptied of their most important contents, empty ones knocked over, glass shattered all over the floor undoubtedly from those who were too late. All that was left were the delicate things, and remnants of those who had been mostly devoured by the zombies Adrian and Charlie had just done away with.

"One day," Adrian muttered. "One day we've been living in this hell, and already it's like this. What is *wrong with people?*"

"Desperate times," Charlie said with a shrug, still far less on edge despite the fact that the two of them had just slaughtered at least fifteen of the undead. "Anyway, we have plenty of food. That's not what we're here for."

"I know, but..." Adrian stopped talking, realizing that she was mad at her husband. He'd managed to stay both safe and sane, but she had to spend the day talking people down from being upset, staying brave, and figuring out how to survive. This wasn't how the two of them normally functioned: in their old lives, *he* was the planner, she usually just made comments to keep others upbeat. Although she hadn't wanted the role of planner, she still had it in her mind that she was the only hope, and was struggling to admit that she needed comfort.

Picking up on how she felt, Charlie hugged her. "Let me take it from here," he said softly. He took her hand and started guiding her to the gardening section.

"Thanks," Adrian managed to say as they walked to where they needed to be. The two of them were hyper aware of everything around them. Any possible sound could mean two things: either their location had been discovered and there were zombies in the store, or there were others who could mistake them for zombies.

Charlie chose to keep his mind off of all the "what ifs" such as "what if we find a little kid who doesn't appear to be hurt and is alone," "suppose we're invaded with another horde past this aisle" and other such unpleasant thoughts. He chose instead to focus on what they were doing, where their final goal was, and appearing to keep it together, to keep Adrian as calm as she could be. Having lived with Adrian for as many years as he had, Charlie was familiar with her body language. He could tell that she was completely in the dark about how scared he actually was. He hoped to keep it this way.

Although the camping section of the store had been picked over for supplies, there was still plenty of bug repellant left, meaning no one else had come up with the cause of the infection.

"See, since the bugs are finally coming out of hiding, I would assume people would have come and bought this anyway," Charlie said to ease the tension a bit.

"I didn't expect there to be this many bottles left," Adrian said plaintively. "We're not going to be able to carry all of this." It hadn't occurred to either of them to pick up a basket or a buggy when they had walked through the doors.

A thought occurred to Charlie, who blurted, "Can you be brave for two seconds? If I run, I can get a basket or two, you'll only have to witness how the store looks on the way out, and it'll be a lot easier to get more goods."

"Does your phone still have power?" Adrian asked, physically and emotionally exhausted. Charlie pulled his phone out of his pocket. It was at 96%. He nodded and dialed her number.

"That feels better," Adrian said as he walked off.

246

Ch. 30
Ace in the Hole

"You're doing a great job," Charlie began as he started back toward the front of the store, taking specific note of what was missing. Food, gone. All of the soap and hand sanitizer, looted. "Let's just be glad I took your advice and stayed in my corner all day so I can handle everything a little easier than you can..."

"You're awesome," she agreed. "Okay but honestly, is there a plan or are you just saying that to keep the rest of us calm?"

Although Adrian wasn't there to see it, she could clearly imagine the grin spreading across Charlie's face as he promised, "There's a plan and you're going to love it. Don't worry about anything; it's completely fool-proof and none of your surviving team is going to disagree with what I have in store."

It crossed her mind that there was an injured party in her team so she looked around for anything that could soothe the broken wrist. It was a good distraction from the fact that she was currently alone.

After about three minutes, Charlie returned, armed not only with two carts, but with two carts filled with as many hand baskets as they could hold. He and his wife hung up their phones, then eyed the carts and shelves filled with bug spray.

"So, can we agree that nobody else realized what caused the infection?" Charlie muttered as they began filling the carts. Adrian put her arm on the shelf top and knocked all of the bottles of bug spray into the cart, making a tremendous crashing noise that would have bothered the both of them on any other day. They'd agreed to create as much of a racket as they could, whatever they did in the store.

That felt good, Adrian thought, her ears ringing with that noise after how quiet her office had been all day. It wasn't a nice feeling, but it was better than the sound of zombie moans.

As Adrian and Charlie continued gathering random supplies, she enjoyed the rush she got every time they picked up anything that they might need, not worrying about the need to pay for it, or thinking they might be picking up too much.

They went around the store, aisle by aisle, stopping anywhere that had anything insect deterrent, food related, hygienic, or even cozy.

"How much food should we stockpile?" Adrian called from the cereal aisle, her basket already about a third full of meticulously arranged boxes of the stuff.

"Don't grab anything that wastes quickly," Charlie answered, two aisles over in canned meat. He never realized there were this many variations of Spam. "Pick up whatever Woody Harrelson would."

"Tallahassee," Adrian corrected him. Charlie had a habit of only referring to movie characters as the actor or actress who played them. She tried breaking him of this habit by always saying the name of the character, but it hadn't worked yet.

Tallahassee's diet wouldn't have been a great idea (it consisted of Twinkies and Twinkies only), but she remembered a line from the book she'd been reading that morning: high-energy, low volume stuff. The book suggested peanuts, which made Adrian suddenly remembered Karl's allergy. She threw all the Boo Berries back on the shelf. The cart also had an assortment of other fruit cereals, but she wasn't sure if they had actual fruits, or just artificial flavors that mocked the fruits. Looking at the goofy drawing on the box, Adrian figured there was no way this children's cereal would have real fruit (she'd probably be safe with the Boo Berries also), and moved to the next aisle.

Adrian had sincerely underestimated how stupid humanity was, as she found the next aisle void of anything, yet pharmacy was still fully stocked. Whoever had been in this store before them had gotten all of the cake, frosting, and bagged chocolates, yet left pain pills and protein shakes. To speed up the looting, she avoided aisles she knew had sweets and cleaned out anything that actually made sense.

Aisle by aisle, product by product, Adrian and Charlie filled their respective carts and hand baskets. They hadn't taken *everything* left in the store, but they had grabbed all the bug spray, pepper spray, and pain killers they could find. The store was still quite well stocked, in contrast to what Adrian had imagined. She figured people would have already gone crazy in here, and aisles and aisles would already be empty.

The store had a totally different feel than what she had expected: years ago, when COVID-19 was a worry, there were no cars in the parking lots, entire shelves in stores had been emptied, and there definitely wasn't any hand sanitizer left. In contrast, today things were simply knocked off of shelves, and sanitation didn't seem to be the number one thing on anyone's mind.

"I think that's it," Adrian panted. Fatigue was genuinely setting in as the adrenaline rush continued to wear off. Keeping a group of journalists alive really took a toll on a person.

Nodding, Charlie led the way toward the front doors. They both did their best to mentally prepare themselves for the stack of corpses that they were about to see again, along with the fact that there might be more. They'd been inside for quite a while, and if there had been more zombies, anyone in their van would have exterminated them.

"It's going to be okay," he told his wife. "There is absolutely no chance that I've been infected, we know you and everyone left in your party are fine, and we've got a big loud van to keep us safe for now."

"Yeah but it gets like a mile to the gallon," Adrian argued, laughing. She was shocked and relieved that she was able to make a joke right now. "Even if it runs out, I have the radio. Which runs on batteries. Which I have a ton of," Charlie reminded her. "Do you see why I love you," she stated, suddenly feeling calmer than she had all day. "I still wish Hank hadn't happened," she muttered. Lucy she had never gotten too close with, Nathan had always been a little *too* rude to her, Hank had really been the main thing that kept her in that job. She hadn't realized how much this loss would affect her until it happened. All day, she couldn't get her mind off of the poor brain damaged man: already borderline suicidal, losing the woman he was in love with had been the final push. Losing the woman he hadn't even ever been on a date with made him completely give up on life. This, paired with his inability to see himself for anything other than someone who would never be able to date anyone at all, was the end.

"Hey," Charlie said, embracing her in a warm hug, "it'll be alright. It was always going to suck, living through any type of apocalypse, let alone one you used to love the idea of, but we always knew it would be difficult. Think about any of the characters you used to love: some of them had their lives falling apart before the big thing happened, others (exactly as you did) lost those who were close to them, but don't take after them. Don't decide you're not okay as they might have, but be within the small percentage of those who push through, making use of the support you have with you."

Crying, Adrian realized how truly overwhelmed she'd been all day. The support from a husband she didn't think she'd ever see again, a group of coworkers now a merry band of misfits in her apocalypse survival story, and a ton of negative emotions clouding all these thoughts.

"You don't have to be the leader anymore, we can all be in charge. All of your team seems to have grasped everything that applies to the leadership position, so you can let them take turns." Now calmed down, she nodded and pulled away from his warm embrace so they could return to the car. This unfortunately became a task more difficult than they had anticipated as they approached the automatic doors which did not respond to their presence.

"Cliché number one," Adrian muttered, miming checking something off of a list. "How *the fuck* do we get out of here now?"

"Can we agree that we were both essentially ready for this day to come?" Charlie asked her. "By which I mean this apocalypse, not necessarily an automatic door that won't open?"

After a short pause, Adrian hesitantly answered with, "I suppose."

Not a second later, Charlie rammed one of the carts into the door, shattering the glass.

"Kind of surprised no one before us had done that," Charlie muttered. He held out a hand and helped Adrian keep her balance.

"How we doing?" Nick asked as they loaded

the back of the car with everything they'd scavenged. He had his eye on a bottle of Aspirin.

"I actually have several presents for you," Adrian answered, noticing where his gaze landed. She pointed out several bags of ice along with a sling that she had found misplaced in the front of the store. That put everyone in a slightly more positive mindset.

After returning Karl's shirt, Denise helped Nick arrange his arm in the sling along with a few ice cubes to numb the pain that had gotten so much worse than before. He didn't dare say anything, since everybody was already so scared, but staying conscious had become a tremendous task.

"I don't know how much longer I can hold on," he finally said. A small part of him was ready to give himself over to the zombies, just so he wouldn't be in pain any longer.

"Um, Denise?" he said hesitantly. "I think maybe I need some sleep, but I'm not sure I'd wake up. I love you and I really don't want this injury to do me in. If I'm going to die, it at least needs to be from the zombies." Denise laughed harder than she had expected at this joke. "Can you talk to me to keep me from falling asleep?

"Of course," she said, giving the side of his head a kiss.

"And don't hold anything back. I want to know it all."

"Well, I hated how stubborn you were about staying with... her. If you'd broken up with your wife a while back—"

"You weren't playfully flirting," Nick interrupted thoughtfully. "You were in love with me and you didn't think you'd ever actually have a shot. We were best friends." Denise looked visibly distressed and a bit embarrassed.

"Everything I said was true," she admitted with a shrug. "Yes, it killed me inside every time you called me 'babe' or I referred to you as 'my one'. We were friends. Yet you, somehow, were the one who initiated our friendly flirting. It was weird."

"I might have gotten some thrill out of it," Nick confessed. Ignoring all safety rules, Denise unbuckled her seat belt and sat on the floor next to him. For Adrian, this brought to mind the 4 rules Columbus had come up with in *Zombieland*. Rule 4: seat belts. Bullshit.

Ch. 31
Capote

With everything now loaded into the van, the car continued to the upcoming unknown location.

Having no idea what they were doing or where they were going, or even if she *wanted* to know those things, Adrian watched all of the buildings they drove by. She noticed that the "mom and pop" shops were still open, but big box stores were closed, full of the undead. After a moment, it occurred to her how this had happened: the managers and bosses had told their more expendable employees to lock up the stores, leaving those people there to eat or be eaten, ultimately.

She needed to not think about this. She climbed into the back of the van to distract herself by taking a roll call. As she said each name, she asked each person how he or she was feeling.

The streets were no less crowded than they'd be on any other day, but none of the other cars were moving. She laughed as Charlie continued to obey traffic laws like using his turn signal, not going 10 miles over the speed limit, and stopping at all lights even though there were clearly no cops around.

Noticing all the abandoned cars on the road, Adrian wondered if the drivers realized what was going on and bolted, were attacked by the undead that had been roaming the streets, or changed, still behind the wheel of their car (the amount of cars run off the road got her to this conclusion).

The effects of the zombie apocalypse were becoming all too clear. In their small town, it wasn't unusual to see people along the road, begging for money. They all had their regular spots, no matter the hour. But today, when the car passed several of the regulars' spots the only thing left seemed to be their abandoned cardboard signs. At one corner, where a gnarly old man always held up his sign "The end is near", there was a sign reading "I told you". It would have been comical, if not for the fact that it was true.

She knew why the people weren't there. It made sense: with no protection, it would have been all too easy for the living dead to turn them or turn them into a fast food meal.

"Obligatory 'does anyone have a sudden urge to eat human flesh?' comment," Adrian said, to which everyone shook their heads once again.

"Okay good. Maybe we should start distributing the bug repellant as we talk?"

"You're the boss," Karl reminded her.

Nodding, she took the bag closest to her and

pulled out a can of Off for herself, then passed the bag around so everyone could do the same.

"So, has Charlie told you anything about where we're going?" Linda asked.

"I didn't ask," Adrian admitted. "And honestly, he was too busy helping me keep my shit together in the store. He probably wouldn't tell any of us anyway. We're all in such fragile states, we'd probably tell him he's crazy."

"Probably true," Trevor agreed. "We've made it this far with just the eight of us and now that we've got someone who went through nothing we did, we kind of have to believe he's going to be able to help us."

"He's kind of our greatest asset," Raleigh piped up. "But yeah Trevor, that was extremely insightful." They laughed to themselves about the fact that the IT guy was keeping it together much more so than the woman who had acted as a company therapist for the past couple of years.

"Um, Adrian," Nancy said sheepishly, "did you remember what you said earlier? About helping me?" Adrian *knew* there was something she was forgetting. "Can you ask Charlie to make a quick stop in Fairborn so I can get my fiancé?" She liked saying it: fiancé. She always knew she'd end up marrying a member of her best friend's family, but she didn't necessarily know it would be to *her*.

Adrian relayed to message to Charlie, who still didn't want to say what he was going to do. "Nope," he answered, shaking his head. "I can't do it. I can't change my plan to get us to Fairborn by stopping in

Fairborn." Adrian laughed; her husband had a sick sense of humor.

"What's the address?" she asked Nancy, who couldn't believe Adrian was actually following through on this. She liked the woman, but hadn't spent enough time with her to know how far she'd go for other people. Especially some random intern. Nancy told her the address and described what the building looked like: it was a fairly plan, tan structure that she and Natalie had lived in for almost two years.

"Okay, so that's taken care of for now. However, I'm exhausted. Does anyone else feel like going to sleep?" Adrian wondered, trying to keep group morale up.

"That sounds like a dumb idea," Nancy muttered, louder than she had anticipated.

"So that's a no from you," Caroline said. "Anyone else?"

"I think I probably should," Karl admitted, mentally kicking himself for not being able to keep his mind in the game. *Nick* wasn't even sleeping. Adrian couldn't help thinking how blissfully peaceful it would be knowing he was asleep and not hearing everything she said, undoubtedly for the sole reason of pointing out why she was incompetent. Before allowing her mind to nourish that thought and build something up inside of her, Adrian simply agreed that he could sleep, provided Caroline keep an eye on him. Anyway, perhaps he would be slightly more pleasant after getting a little bit more rest: they felt a little more secure being in the van and no longer felt the need to sleep in shifts.

None of the others in the van felt that tired, either being too on edge to think they could or feeling plenty rested from the sleep they'd gotten earlier. They all sat back to find out what the ultimate plan was going to be.

Knowing their next destination, nobody was surprised when the car pulled onto the expressway leading out of town. None of the survivors in the car had much cared for Springfield and wouldn't have minded relocating at some point in time, but never thought they'd be leaving because of a zombie apocalypse.

There are never many cars on the road at quarter after 5 in the morning, aside from the unfortunate people who had early morning or late night jobs and were just getting to or just leaving work. Never before had any of them seen this many cars run off the road or crashed into each other with no road crews around to help, which further added to the tenseness of the situation. As badly as they all were trying to manage their emotions and be happy that they still had their health and one another, the more time went on, the worse they all got.

The eerie feeling was heightened when they noticed many clear signs that something was going on. There were still things that seemed completely undisturbed: the road signs marking what highway they were on, the signs showing how far to the next city or the nearest fast food joint were spotless, no blood, no bullet holes like Adrian was used to seeing in films, no stacks of human intestines surrounding them.

"I hate this," Raleigh muttered, crossing her arms in both anger and defeat.

"What's going on?" Adrian asked, stressing that the one person who did the most to help her keep it together was about to fall apart.

"When I applied for this job, nowhere in the job description did it read, 'Helping your coworkers in the case of a zombie apocalypse.' This is way more than I am qualified to help with."

"Fine print," came Karl's voice, practically as if he were talking in his sleep.

"Talk to me," Adrian said. "You need a distraction, so how about a breach of protocol? Did Hank, in fact, ever come talk to you about his life?"

"Oh, all the time," Raleigh said, making absolutely no indication of her hesitancy to talk about him earlier in the night. "Yeah, he hated his job. Not only did he work so far away from Lucy, but he *really* couldn't talk to her. Of course it was all in his head, and we were working on some strategies for him to use whenever he felt particularly bad about the way he looked, but his mind really couldn't digest what it needed to digest." She made to keep talking, but sighed and admitted, "And you probably shouldn't know the rest."

"No, I want to. Please. Hank was a good friend, and I really need closure. I need to know everything there is to know about him."

"You're sure?" Raleigh checked. Adrian nodded, so the counselor said, "The rest of you may want to not listen. For one it may not be interesting, plus it's a really tragic tale. *Really* tragic." She was half concerned she wouldn't be able to make the words to tell the story.

"He really loved Lucy," Raleigh went in. "We can all agree on this, right?" There were nods of agreement around the van, so she continued, "Right. Everyone at the company knew this except for the one person who *needed* to know: Lucy herself. Hank had this little voice in his head (not a literal one, I was treating him for emotions not mental issues) that kept telling him Lucy would never talk to him let alone give him the time of day. We'd been working for the past four months on strategies to help him silence that voice when he spoke to Lucy. He'd made contact with her a few times in the past three or four weeks, casual 'hey's and 'how you doing?'s."

The pit that had been forming in Adrian's stomach all day grew. She had a feeling she knew how this story was going to end. His relationship with Lucy was far more advanced than Adrian had known, although she did not yet know the full extent of it. Raleigh stopped for a moment in order to prepare herself to deliver the final blow that would break Adrian in a whole new way.

"It happened yesterday," Raleigh narrated. "The game changer. He had asked her to spend some time with him outside of work. She'd agreed."

The entire scene replayed in Adrian's head, but this time how it would have looked from Hank's point of view: Lucy passing out, how it must have looked seeing her trying to fix the issue, and then woman staggering out the door. And of course *she* had been the one to tell everyone it happened.

Ch. 32
Charlie Wilson's War

"I had no idea," Adrian said. "I thought Hank hadn't even said two words to her."

"I told him not to let anyone know because it would add to the pressure he was already feeling," Raleigh explained to her. "I wanted him to go on like he had always been on his own time, just not when Lucy was around."

He'd clearly done a very good job at achieving that goal, as this news came as a complete shock to everyone in the van. Before the zombies and the death of her friend, Adrian remembered him telling her that he hadn't gotten anywhere in terms of talking with her.

It would have been so much better to find this out from Hank. If Lucy were still alive and healthy. Now that they're both gone completely, one of them living wouldn't have been important. If Lucy hadn't been bitten by a mosquito and turned into a flesh eating zombie, Hank wouldn't have had any reason to be upset and would have lived. After thinking through this, Adrian realized she had no real way of knowing whether or not her close work friend would have eventually become exactly what Lucy had been, being as he and the woman had apparently been spending a fair amount of time with one another and there was no sure way yet to know for certain that the infection wasn't airborne. She doubted it was, given they'd been safe in her small office and the inside of this vehicle, but had no way of knowing how long Lucy had been infected and what of it may have come off on Hank.

On the other hand, he'd still been Hank, behaving in the exact same manner as Adrian had known him to from the moment the two had become friends, up until his overreacting to Lucy's change and meeting his demise. Of course, just because he had been behaving normally didn't mean he wouldn't have changed eventually; that was something Adrian knew she was going to have to think about a lot in order to get over this loss. There was always the possibility that any of them would change, but Adrian forced those incredibly unwelcome and unnecessary thoughts out of her mind and focused instead on the fact that they were going somewhere and were going to be safer than they'd been in the past day.

"How is Karl?" Adrian asked, trying to keep her mind off of Hank. "And Nick, how are you?"

"I'm not convinced Karl's *asleep*, but I think he's okay," Caroline answered. She had been keeping a close eye on him and noticing no change in his breathing pattern or the way he was holding himself. She was right, he was not asleep and absolutely fine, but he so badly wanted to be asleep that he wasn't about to let them know he was awake and fully aware of what they were discussing. He also knew Adrian would go off on him if he did. He'd known he wouldn't be able to get any sleep the moment he closed his eyes and saw flashes of everything that had happened, but it was nice to relax with them thinking he was trying to sleep as they weren't going to ask him to do anything. With any luck, he figured he could keep this charade up until they got to wherever it was that Charlie was taking them.

"At least he's being quiet," Adrian muttered, giving Karl the answer he needed as to whether or not it was alright he wasn't doing anything. She'd noticed that he wasn't snoring and decided he therefore must have just been pretending at the moment. "And he was definitely being himself before 'going to sleep' so we feel safe from him. And how are you, Nick?"

"In pain," he answered. "But if I went to sleep, I'd probably never wake up, so not doing that. Plus I have a girlfriend." Denise was astonished at how brave he was being been, considering the amount of pain he must have been in from the moment that he slipped.

"You really should have let us know how bad you were," Linda said, thinking she could have given him more ice or at least been more careful about making sure the ice didn't hurt him. "I had no idea."

"It wasn't that bad at first," Nick said. "Remind us how many times it made you vomit?" Linda argued. The longer this went on, the higher tensions got. Adrian didn't know any of these people well, and as they were only just getting to know each other, they really needed to keep their heads on straight.

"How are we doing back there?" Charlie called, as if aware that Adrian was going through a difficult stream of thoughts. His voice was barely audible over the roar of the van's engine, but the fact that he was still thinking about her calmed Adrian's nerves just enough that she was able to articulate how she was feeling.

"Same old," Adrian answered with a shrug. "No one knows what's going on and there's always the possibility of the shit hitting the fan, but we've distributed the insect repellant, so there's that."

"Why are we going to Fairborn?" Raleigh asked, now that Charlie was conversing with the team. "Surely going to a larger town than ours is an awful idea..."

"Well, for one, there's Nancy's situation," he said. "Plus, I wanted to get us out of Springfield. We already know there are zombies there. I think that a bigger town would be more likely to have people teaming up to help one another to survive, much like the group of you did."

"You were always going to take us to Fairborn," Adrian pondered. "Remind me why?"

"Well there's almost the entirety of both of our families there," Charlie said. "And originally we were supposed to be there tonight anyway."

"But how is it going to keep us safe?" Adrian demanded. She loved Charlie, but he had a bad habit of trying to turn things into what they really weren't.

"You know that forest near where your parents live?" Charlie said to her. Adrian knew exactly the one he was speaking of; it had next to nothing in it, was always covered in mud, and really needed some a major upgrade.

When they were young, most of the kids in Fairborn made a game of daring one another to go into those woods during the dark of night and stay for a set period of time without being so scared that they had to leave. They all believed their parents and other family members knew nothing about the game, when in reality the adults were all too aware of it. They let it go because nothing dangerous lurked in those woods.

"So you're taking us to the most deserted part of town," Adrian summarized. "*Assuming*, of course, that no one else has had this idea."

The second part came out slightly harsher than she had meant it to, but Charlie had no trouble brushing past that. He explained to his wife that yes, that was the plan. He added that this way they would also be able to stop by to see how her parents were faring.

"But what do we do once we get to the woods?" Raleigh wanted to know. "It's not like we can just feel safe camping out, waiting for this all to pass; weather is going to change, this van is going to run out of gas, and we can't stay like that forever."

"Nor will we have to," Charlie let her know, unable to stop himself from grinning about how cunning his plan was turning out. "We'll be totally safe in a place that no one would even think about."

"That fucking warehouse," Adrian deadpanned. "We're going to that warehouse they never sold, aren't we?"

"Think about it," Charlie said, unable to hide his excitement, "it's in a remote location and there's only one road leading to it."

Charlie had always made the comment that it was the perfect place to go in the case of the zombie apocalypse, but of course those had always just been jokes. It had the benefits of being made out of concrete, it was large enough to comfortably house all the members they had in their party, and, by nightfall, it would be completely hidden.

"Well he's not wrong," Adrian said to everyone in the back of the van. She knew that had Karl been awake (or not pretending he wasn't), he would have made a remark about how she should have thought of this plan a long time ago. She didn't want to think it, but her own mind couldn't help going there.

Ch. 33
Fear and Loathing in Las Vegas

"How much longer?" Denise asked. Even though Nick was awake, his face had become a shade of green that she didn't like.

"Shouldn't be long now," Adrian said passively, noting the sign that Fairborn was only 11 miles away. "Charlie's been driving pretty fast anyway, so we should at least get to the town in just a couple of minutes. Keep watching the road signs, if it makes you feel any better." Charlie had finally stopped caring about road safety.

Glancing at the dashboard, Denise took note of the fact that he was going 90 in what should have been a 70 MPH zone. Having been the "reassuring voice" for so much of the day, Adrian was a little sick of having to take care of everybody's emotions. This thought, though, gave her an idea of a place closer than the warehouse that maybe could have been a safe place to go.

"Charlie!" she called over the roar of the engine. "Stop the car and turn it off." Pulling to the side of the expressway, Charlie turned off the van and turned toward her.

"What's up?" he asked, hoping the conversation would be quick: the van was off and quiet. Adrian was speaking in a hushed tone and there wasn't anything beside the uneven ground to keep the zombies away. It had crossed Charlie's mind, also, that perhaps they shouldn't be as careful about the guy with the sprained or broken wrist and just let the zombies take him. Couldn't be much worse than how he was feeling right now.

"As great an idea as the warehouse is," Adrian said, "there's also that old Air Force base. It will probably have things that would be useful for our survival like stored water and rations. And the sooner we all have a chance to rest up without worrying about getting attacked, the better. If we stop there, we can get the sleep we need, and the rest of us can scavenge for supplies."

"We can *try* that," he agreed, starting the van again. "Almost there. And we'll go to Nancy's after we decide if that's safe."

As promised, it wasn't long before the sign reading "Exit 4" came up. Charlie slowed down and took the off-ramp. They passed an old drive-in theater, the one where Adrian and Charlie had had many dates together, leaving them both thinking about those good times instead of this bad one they were in now.

Adrian thought back to the first time Charlie

had taken her there: they both knew they were only going so they wouldn't have to hook up at either of their parents' places. They weren't there to watch the movie. They'd asked the man at the ticket booth for a ticket to whatever was starting next so they wouldn't have to wait any longer than necessary before they could get intimate.

The next movie that was being screened was *Dawn of the Dead.* Two people who had a mutual love of zombies, no matter what they might have planned, can't go to a theater playing a zombie movie and not watch it. They split a popcorn and discussed movie, talking about the realism of the violence and what they would do if they ever found themselves in this situation. The fact that it was a "what if" all those years ago almost made her laugh. She wondered if Charlie remembered them having that discussion.

"*Dawn of the Dead,*" Charlie said with a laugh.

"We were so young," Adrian added, glad she wasn't the only one who found this situation interesting. She couldn't even remember any of the things they had come up with in their zombie apocalypse plan, aside from making sure the two of them stuck together. "Our plan didn't exactly work though, did it?"

"I think we both know that plan was absolute rubbish," Charlie said. "We were, what, fifteen at the time?"

"Eighteen," Adrian corrected him, hoping he remembered more about what they came up with than she did.

Ignoring this minor interrupted, Charlie continued, "Firstly, you were all the way across town when we found out the apocalypse was on us, and we had completely planned on it being just the two of us against everyone else in the world already being infected. We weren't going to trust anyone, and we were going to do exactly what you had me do all of today: hide in the basement and wait everything out."

"It was fun, though," Adrian reminded him. "You and me and a zombie movie, talking about what we both loved."

She tried to put her mind back to the days when she thought this would be cool, not life-threatening and beyond horrific, but struggled. She could understand how she might have thought this would be a cool adventure, but every time a positive thought about the situation started to form, it would be crushed with a memory of one of the worse things that had just happened. Karl's rudeness, watching Lucy eat the corpse (it didn't help that she didn't even know whose it was), losing Hank... There was simply no way of denying that the bad far outweighed the good. Nothing about this was as fun as it was watching actors playing characters going through it on the screen, or reading about in books.

Unable to understand why in the hell the two of them were having this discussion, Caroline interrupted them. "When should we start waking him up?" she asked of Karl.

"I think you should take care of Karl," Adrian

said without hesitation. Knowing Karl wasn't asleep, Caroline didn't even bother coaxing him awake. She just deadpanned, "Wake up."

"So we're going to an abandoned warehouse, then?" Karl said. His sudden reanimation made it clear that although he didn't sleep, he still got the rest that he needed. "Okay."

"Are we *sure* he's not infected?" Adrian muttered, noticing how easy-going Karl had suddenly become. Although she said it as a joke, she *was* a bit confused at his sudden change of attitude. Nobody said anything, so she tried to not let herself get worked up about it.

"I'm done arguing," Karl admitted with a shrug. "As long as this plan works, that is." So that tarot reading was right.

Adrian felt better now that he sounded like the Karl that she was used to. The tension that had built up in her body began to loosen as the familiar surroundings of the town where she grew up unfolded around her. She allowed her mind to wander off to reminisce about what life had been like when she was younger and before any of this had happened. She and her friends always loved spending time downtown, specifically Foy's Halloween Stores, which was open year round and had a whole strip of places they loved to hang out. They'd spend some time at the Halloween Shop, which was filled floor to ceiling with creepy costumes and decorations, then head to the children's costume shop that had opened once the business expanded (oddly, the adult costume shop had opened first), ending their trip with a stop at the Rock-n-Roll Grill, which had really inexpensive hand made food that was always a good way to end the day. Every October, they would also add a trip to the Haunted House Store, which had different tours one could take, and a really creepy execution scene in the back. Adrian used to love the fake screams of the dummy, but now cringed, thinking about how she used to get enjoyment from such things.

As they passed by the old Valeno gas station where Adrian always would stop to fuel her car when she came to visit her parents, she checked how the gas gauge was looking. Though there wasn't a ton of gas left in the tank, it didn't seem an incredibly smart time to stop since their safe haven was so close, so they simply rolled past it, knowing the Air Force base wasn't far.

Familiar though all of these surroundings were, they were now littered with exactly the same awful things they'd seen on the streets of Springfield: blood, dead bodies, car wrecks, cars with dead bodies that would undoubtedly soon become zombies, and reanimated corpses. Barely recognizable as the place in which she had grown up. She forced herself to believe that everything was going to be okay, they were only going to be in this part of town for a few minutes, and to focus on the things they had going for them.

Alright Chase, she told herself, oddly reminding herself of the boss they had lost earlier in the day, *you can do this. The base isn't far from here, and you know this place well. There's food, a community has been built among all of us, and this isn't going to kill you. Keep it together.* She forced herself to look away from the windows displaying the horrors lurking just outside. It was a difficult task given the natural human urge to observe gore and know about how much bad there is going on in the world. After growing up as a horror nerd, she knew it had to do with the release of dopamine in the brain, which was just habit for her as she was used to enjoying seeing these type of things. She picked a spot on the carpet of the van they were in to look at, a neon green speck which really stood out on the otherwise black carpet.

Despite how much useless conversation had happened throughout the day as they hid in the News Sun building, everybody decided to stay silent for the remainder of the trip. Whether this was due to emotions, fear, or starting to get tired of one another, nobody knew. The next time Adrian looked up, it was as the van turned onto the street where the Air Force base was located.

The place was arranged rather strangely; it had almost no signs pointing toward it, causing many confused patrons who thought they were on a road to end up in a line leading into the exhibit which sat on top of a base that contained a museum in the back.

Once the car had made its way around all of the dead things cluttering up the street leading to the front door, another obstacle came up: they weren't the only ones who had thought to use this as a safe place. It was already infested, but with raccoons.

Charlie hated raccoons, so he stopped the car and they all looked at each other.

"Well?" Adrian asked.

"I mean, don't they usually avoid people?" he asked. "Which makes it weird that I'm so phobic of them, anyway." The issue was there were tens of the animal, maybe hundreds, but the building they had come up to was more of a garage than anything, so he decided it was alright to simply drive the van forward.

"This is a terrible idea," Denise said. "We wouldn't know—" She stopped mid sentence as the yellow eyes looked at everybody through the dark tunnel. There weren't tens or hundreds, in fact there were very few. But the few that there were had all mutated into something else.

The virus was infecting animals as well. Even though having Charlie let Dwight go had crushed him and Adrian, they now understood that it was better this way and he wouldn't have been the snuggly bunny they had both come to know and love. He probably now looked a lot like these raccoons: a higher than average number of eyes, fur falling off in chunks, and same as human zombies, they'd been feeding off the flesh of their own kind. Adrian didn't know if all the raccoons had gathered here to avoid the zombie ones, or the zombie ones had started here, but it didn't matter. These things all had the virus, and nobody cared to find out if they'd also eat human flesh.

Ch. 34
Killing Fields

Although everybody was safe in the van, looking at the hundreds of eyes and mutilated bodies caused sheer terror. For Adrian, it was reminiscent of finding Lucy earlier in the day, taking her time eating the dead coworker.

"I knew those things were assholes," Charlie muttered, throwing the van into reverse.

"That was... pretty much our last hope," Adrian said as Charlie backed out the way they came. "Why would they—"

"It seems unlikely, but maybe wild animals know something is wrong," Trevor interrupted. "Pretend you're a squirrel or a raccoon or whatever, and you're going about your day, doing your thing, when all of a sudden you get jumped. You might think it's a prey, but then realize it's one of you. Why wouldn't another sentient being do the same as we did and hide?"

"And they stayed together for survival," Linda added. "Like us, they made a team. That's why they were all raccoons and not any variety of animals."

"I hated that," Charlie said with a shudder. He asked Adrian to make sure that everyone was back in the van.

"So what now?" Adrian deadpanned. "If we go to the warehouse and it's the same way, what happens?"

"You should rest," Charlie told her. She got really worked up and anxious when she stressed too much, and right now she'd had beyond too much. "Close your eyes at least until we get to Nancy's place."

She knew he was right and reluctantly adjusted the seat so it was leaning back. She closed her eyes hoping that the bad images wouldn't come flooding her mind.

Adrian realized she must have drifted off, because when she woke up, they were at an apartment complex. Must have been Nancy's.

The second the van stopped moving, Nancy bolted to open the door. Raleigh jumped in front of her, knowing the only thing on Nancy's mind was getting inside, but not knowing whether or not the undead might be swarming inside the building.

"What, did you think it was totally okay to just leave us and get yourself killed?" Karl asked a Nancy that already felt bad about what might have happened.

"Babe!" Caroline said, trying to distract him. "Listen, we're all upset right now; she doesn't need you adding to it." Nothing was more important to Nancy than getting inside to be with Natalie, but as she pushed Karl out of the way, doors to the building started opening. She didn't feel overly concerned, as it was mostly senior citizens who lived on the bottom floor, but as porch doors opened both downstairs and upstairs, she realized age didn't matter to zombies. She saw Ruth, the old lady who had cooked brownies when she heard Nancy had finally broken up with Scott, now not the same person: her jaw was only hanging on by a thread, she was covered in her own blood and the blood of others, and though she no longer had quite the same limp she'd had for the past few years, she wasn't moving like a human.

Next she noticed Luke, the pretentious businessman, stepping onto his balcony from one of the second floor apartments. For the first time in the two years Nancy had lived there, she got to see him not wearing a suit, but a pair of boxers and an old t-shirt. It was arguably weirder than the fact that he was a zombie. The creature walked back and forth on the balcony a few times, then must have realized it was the only thing there as it leaned over the balcony railing, then tumbled, landing in a heap on the lawn directly beneath the balcony. Nancy froze, waiting for the zombie to stand up, which it did mere seconds after landing.

After Nancy processed what was happening right in front of her, in *her* apartment building, she grabbed both of the steak knives they'd gotten from the kitchen, put a bottle of bug spray under her arm, and shoved the van's door open. Caroline, Linda and

Karl wasted no time grabbing whatever they could carry that might help, realizing Nancy wasn't very clear headed, and noticing all of the porch doors slowly opening, only zombies stepping out.

"No," Nancy told them. She had a certain stubborn streak that only came in handy on occasion. "I need to do this." Ignoring the fact that they were ignoring her and were following not far behind, Nancy went to what used to be Luke and sprayed him in the face with her can of bug spray. The body fell quickly, but Nancy wasn't satisfied. The anger coursing through her body made her almost as deadly as the zombies, but she knew it was alright because it was for survival and she'd never kill a human. These things didn't have souls or any type of mind, so there was less than zero reason for them to survive.

She had a clear path to the front door of her apartment building, but she knew Ruth had walked behind it, and if there were two, there were bound to be more. Knowing she had at least three other humans there, she followed the path she'd seen Ruth walk, fully intending to take her out, regardless of how the zombie reacted to seeing her.

Ruth had gotten surprisingly far for an older zombie, but had found someone who was still alive, as she was crouched a body, her face buried in the stomach as she tore guts out with one hand, feeding them to herself using the other. Nancy could see the blood spattered on the grass, running down the woman's nightgown she rarely changed out of.

Nancy successfully snuck up behind her, and

dug the knife into the old woman's back. It was still a bit sad, seeing this dear old lady not only covered in the blood of... 38B, but knowing there was no hope for her. Nancy hadn't spoken to Natalie in a bit, which definitely wasn't helping her stay sane, as she sat on the floor and dug the knife into the old woman's body over and over, making sure the zombie wouldn't come back, and if it was still alive, it knew how she felt about it.

As she pulled back a fifth time, the knife was snatched out of her hand, leaving her defenseless should the corpse have come back. She warily looked over her shoulder at who (or what) had taken it and saw Linda, looking very concerned.

"Come on," she said, gently lifting Nancy by the arm. "We should get you inside." She stood up slowly and the two of them started to the front door, which Nancy should have just done in the first place.

The front door of the apartment building didn't lock, so Nancy pulled it open and followed Linda in. They both really wanted to get to Nancy's place, but were forced instead to wait for Raleigh and Karl to finish off the other zombies that had either stepped out from their apartments or fallen from the upper balcony. It *was* better to have more than two people per group. "You take the front, I'll watch in here," Nancy said, knowing that the amount of porch doors was nothing compared to the number in the hallway.

Seconds after agreeing to that, doors inside the hallway began to open. Nancy had used up a lot of energy just on Ruth, but knew that if any of the things that might be about to be crowding the hallway came at her, she couldn't back down. First, she had to take care of the couple who had emerged from apartment 2, who had invited her and Natalie over for a party the other day. She suddenly felt bad about declining the invite, having had a relatively bad day at work. Doing nothing and yet still getting yelled at by Nathan didn't seem so bad now that he'd become a zombie, nor did going to a sparsely attended party that wouldn't be interesting at all.

Being ambidextrous, she put herself in the very risky position of standing between the two who were now making their way closer and closer, so that she could spray one in the face with the bug spray, and stab the other in the face with a knife. Her apartment was about halfway down the hall, and she wanted to get there as fast as physically possible. It never even occurred to her to only deal with one of the zombies and let any of the other three people help her.

As Nancy attacked these two, she didn't notice any of the other three, also busy killing those who had wandered into the hallway. She didn't notice Karl, who (much like Nancy) was only focused on getting back safely because of his new relationship status, making use of the hammer he'd grabbed from Charlie's stash of possible weapons and slamming it into the face of the Power Rangers fanatic (John) who'd staggered out of his apartment the second he smelled something alive in the hallway. Nancy was close friends with this individual and knew all of his opinions about the show, along with the fact that he thought the film that came out in 2017 was terrible, as it didn't show the Rangers with the same traits they'd had in the original series.

Karl bashed this man's face in, recoiling as the foul smell he thought he'd be used to by now emerged from the mess. He stepped back, yanking the hammer with him, trying to ignore the bits of skin that were now sticking to it. Since they would undoubtedly be encountering many more zombies on their way down the hall, if not on the way back, he forced himself to not let it bother him and check to see how everybody else was doing. He saw Caroline, holding up the Zombie Strike sniper rifle, both of her hands shaking uncontrollably. There was no way she'd be able to hit the zombie that was quickly advancing on her.

The good news is it was a zombie and "quickly" didn't exactly describe how it moved. It was incredibly clumsy, but Karl was concerned regardless. Moving so fast that the zombie *and* Caroline couldn't process what he was doing, Karl pushed her out of the path while also snatching the gun, and shot the zombie five times in the head. It seemed like an incredible over exaggeration, but the guy went down.

"Thanks, babe," Caroline panted, realizing how panicked she'd become. Karl wouldn't have done so much for anyone else in the group, but to him, Caroline was perfection and there was no way he'd let her down. "But what the hell is this guy wearing?" Karl hadn't processed how oddly the zombie had been dressed, but took a moment to check it out. The body was wearing a mustard yellow button down top, grey green tie (appropriate for a zombie, Karl supposed), and a casual green suit, the outfit finished off by a pair of overly dorky glasses. As Karl tried to piece it together, Nancy walked over, drenched in sweat from nerves and overexertion.

"Dwight Schrute," she panted. "He was working on his Dwight Schrute cosplay. He wore his new cosplays for days at a time to try to get into character. He did it professionally."

"We're sure he wasn't cosplaying zombie Dwight, correct?" Karl wanted to make sure.

Meanwhile, Linda was trying to focus on a personal goal, hoping it would give her the push she needed to get in, get out, and get back to the van. She knew that it helped her to focus on one concrete thing to get through things, and chose Trevor, inventing a story that he'd be disappointed if she got herself killed.

Her weapon of choice for this trip was one of the handheld Nerf guns, but she was hoping she wouldn't have to use it. Naturally, hoping for this doesn't usually go well when you're in the midst of a zombie apocalypse, and sure enough, within minutes of entering the building, what appeared to be a young adult holding some nice looking fabric was staggering up to her, looking hungry. It looked to be having more trouble walking than any of the others they'd encountered, though. A quick glance at it explained the problem: one leg was significantly shorter than the other, a condition that must have occurred when it accidentally sliced its foot off, probably with a pair of scissors or a rotary cutter.

Shoot for the head, Linda reminded herself, raising the gun to the creature. She was much more focused than Caroline, whose mind had simply shut down at the prospect of dealing with another zombie.

It took two shots to down this creature, the first missing it and zooming by the thing's head completely. The second shot was square in the forehead, taking it out. She remembered a lesson from movies, though, and then stood over the body, shooting it twice more. She gathered the four bullets she'd shot and dropped them into a pocket, regretting her decision to not stay in the van.

"Ashely, too," Nancy said from behind her. Linda jumped, thinking Nancy was still across the hall with Caroline, wondering if she just knew every person in the building. "Damn. That one hurts. She was cool; paying her way through college with this really cool online craft shop. She made custom shirts and pillowcases. I've ordered a few. They're overpriced, but Natalie likes when I wear nerdy stuff."

"Can we just get out of here?" Linda said through gritted teeth. She'd forgotten how forceful these things got over time, and hadn't considered how long they'd be out of the van.

"I'm just a few more doors down," Nancy said, walking faster, both for her sake and Linda's. She stopped in front of a door and tried to turn the knob. It didn't budge. She and Natalie always left it unlocked, since it was a relatively low crime area, but of course Natalie would have locked it given what Nancy had called to tell her. Knowing full well she didn't have her key because she never did, Nancy checked her pockets anyway.

Karl and Raleigh were just catching up as Nancy gave in, realizing she was going to have to knock to be let in to her own apartment. She thought about all the scraping at the door throughout the day in Adrian's office and knew she'd have to be clear if she wanted to be let in. She knocked quickly 5 times to the tune of "shave and a haircut" and was going to knock the "two bits" part, when the door opened. "Two bits?" Scott said, opening the door. Before Nancy could react, he opened the door wide and invited the group to come in and decompress.

With the exception of Nancy, everybody went in and sat on the couch in the living room. Nancy, on the other hand, went directly to her fiancé to catch up on the day and current state of events.

"I hope you don't mind that I had Scott come over," was the first thing Natalie said. "It's just... if what you said was true, and... he's my baby brother and I needed to know he was okay." Natalie was a full five and a half hours older than Scott, and never let him forget the fact.

"Natalie, I love you, and if you needed Scott to be here in order to stay sane, it's alright," Nancy responded. She couldn't recall the last time she'd been as happy as she was in this moment, however, finally back with the person she belonged with. As much as Adrian had promised this would happen, she didn't want to get her hopes too high.

Although Nancy had broken up with Scott, she was already rather close with the family, so she still saw him at birthdays, holidays, and celebrations. Their breakup hadn't been outwardly messy (Scott was actually quite happy for the two), and breakups are just inherently bad, but the two of them were perfectly civil to each other."But we really need to get going. As happy as I am, it's not safe here. Not at all." Another reason Nancy didn't think she'd see Natalie again was their porch door: it was mostly glass, rarely locked, and completely not zombie proof.

"You're sure? You don't want to break up now?" Natalie said, a recurring joke between the two.

"Yeah, totally. Right after asking you to marry me," Nancy replied, trying to figure out their best way back to the van. "But before that, let's all get out of here through the porch door." Admittedly, not any more or less safe than going down the hall again, but she really didn't want to see the dead zombies they'd left in the hallway. Especially Ashley.

The two women returned to the rest of the group, inquiring whether or not everybody else was feeling up to heading out. Nancy explained the issue of safety, causing a resounding agreement that it was time to go.

"Zombies?" Scott asked as they exited through the porch door, each partnered up with another. Natalie scrunched her face.

"I... I didn't tell him," she admitted to Nancy,

walking fast. The stretch between the exit of the apartment and the van was a lawn that, in truth was only about ten yards, but felt like an entire football field. "I didn't want him to be too scared to come over, so I told him you asked me to marry you. I've had the curtain pulled over the porch door window all day, closed all of the blinds—"

"And he's surprisingly oblivious," Nancy finished for her. "Probably thought there were flash mobs or something."

"I can hear you," Scott called from two groups back. Nancy and Natalie chuckled, always quick to get under his skin, and trying to not focus on the fact that they were rushing to a van during an apocalypse. Anyway, they were engaged now, and it felt more important to look at the positives.

Inside the van, everybody saw the group hurrying to get back to safety. Nobody quite understood their escape routine, but there weren't any zombies around (maybe the majority of senior citizens who lived there didn't come back, but why speculate?) and leaving this area felt like a smart plan.

Nick and Denise sat in the back of the van, where Nick was able to prop his arm on the cup holder to stop it from moving until the van took off again, and Denise continued to talk and make sure he didn't fall asleep. Adrian and Charlie were still in the front, Charlie gripping the steering wheel ready to drive at a moment's notice. Adrian had drifted off again, and Charlie did not want to disturb her unless it was necessary. Raleigh and Karl were in the main seats in the van, Raleigh perched to open the door, and it looked like her moment was coming. The second the team got to the van, Raleigh had the door open and ready for them to jump in.

Nobody even bothered sitting in the seats, but as the door slammed shut, Charlie took off, driving across town to their final stop. The people in the back situated themselves in whatever configuration made the most sense: Nick took his arm off of where it was resting, as the road was uneven and he knew it was going to just jolt the injury. Scott had joined the two of them in the back, always trying to inconvenience people in the least way possible, aware that it wasn't anyone's favorite spot and that his sister and ex-girlfriend would just want to spend time together in the open space on the floor. Raleigh was still situated on the chair by the sliding door, sitting across from Karl, who now had Caroline sitting cross legged in front of him, holding the wall for safety.

Nancy and Natalie were sitting in the open space in the front of the van, both trying to come down from the adrenaline rush of knowing that at any point from the apartment to the van, they could have been killed. Natalie thought about the fact that Nancy had been through a lot of situations throughout the day, and forced herself to be okay. "Kiss me," she said, stroking Nancy's arm. It hadn't even occurred to Nancy that she hadn't done that since getting back, but she really needed it.

"Our first kiss as an engaged couple," Nancy said, playing with Natalie's hair as she leaned in.

Their kiss was incredible; neither woman thought they could have another kiss that felt as good as their first, but after spending the day thinking they'd never see each other again, it was just as intense and reminded both of why and how much they loved each other at a whole different level.

"That was nice," breathed Natalie as they parted. "I love you so much."

"I love you, too," Nancy said. She still hadn't had a chance to find out why Adrian had put so much effort into getting them back together, but she could never find a way to thank her enough for it.

"Fuck!" Scott blurted, snapping both women out of their nice moment. "Shit, you weren't lying, there are fucking *zombies* in the street!" He saw five depressed looking people outside, walking aimlessly with poor posture, covered in blood. On any other day, it would seem that they were sad, looking for a place in life, but there was blood all over their bodies; both black and red, and their skin was very pale. He hadn't seen this as he'd driven to Nancy and Natalie's place earlier in the day, which he realized was because he'd been blaring music with the windows down, trying to feel cool.

"Settle down," Nancy told him. "We have *a lot* to catch up on." As Nancy recounted the events of the day to him (taking particular care to mention her rushed engagement to Natalie), he thought back to several peculiar things that had happened throughout the day.

"That wasn't a package delivery," he observed once Nancy had told him everything. "Natalie, you liar!" She shrugged innocently.

"I figured my phone dying and me getting a new one delivered was easier to digest than there being zombies outside," she explained. "And that moaning? Yes, there's a new virus going around, but it isn't exactly the kind that you lie in bed and complain about. Those were zombies in the hall."

After all this time, she was *still* stuck up about having been born before he was and always trying to protect him. He appreciated it in this case, but normally it pissed him off to no end.

292

Ch. 35
Live from Baghdad

The city around them was full of zombies, all seeming to move individually. Charlie knew from his and Adrian's movie nights that this wasn't normal behavior; they liked to travel in groups. He wasn't going to complain that there weren't any mobs, but it was... weird. Damn near unnatural.

They reached a neighborhood area, which looked entirely normal, save for the zombies mindlessly milling about. There wasn't much blood, the trash bins were all out on the curb as they normally would be, and people's gardens had clearly been worked on when beautification was still important.

Pushing all of this out of his head, Charlie drove, pulling into the driveway of a very familiar house. "One quick break before safety," Charlie said, gently shaking Adrian awake. It took a moment for her to get out of her sleepy haze to realize where they were: her parents'.

The house looked completely normal from where they were sitting: no blood was splattered on the front windows, all of the lights still seemed to be on, but the inside might tell an entirely different story. The light in the kitchen even appeared to still be on. She wanted to leave it like this, not be stuck with whatever it truly was as her last memory there.

Adrian voiced her concerns, but decided that she needed to know if her parents were still alive inside. Even if something *had* happened to her parents, she didn't think she could feel much worse than she already did.

"I think we should all go together," Adrian announced, noting some movement in the trees surrounding the house. "Keep one another in check and sane. It's probably safe, and it's conceivable that there are supplies in the house that we can use."

"I don't want Nick going out there," Denise argued. He shook his head, trying to argue that he was fine, but Denise took it as him not wanting to join either.

"Fine, whatever," Adrian agreed, trying to expedite the process so she'd know what was happening faster. "You guys stay here."

"Can I have more drugs?" Nick murmured.

"I'm really sorry Nick!" Denise cried, grabbing one of the bottles of pills. "I should have given these to you already! I'm a bad person." Her voice trailed off at the end. "We'll stay here while they go inside and see if there's anything we can salvage. Then we'll try to find a real safe place." The house already seemed like a dangerous place to be, as several zombies were already coming out of the shadows, undoubtedly having smelled the newcomers.

"Cool," Nick agreed, still groggy and in pain. "Can I get some more ice." Denise gave him another chunk and waited as he set it where it would be most helpful.

"Okay, but you realize that with you guys all here worrying, this car is now surrounded with them," Nick said. He got passive aggressive when he was overwhelmed. Without realizing it, everyone in the van had gotten very quiet hoping Nick was going to be okay to continue on, which was especially inviting for those in Fairborn who had already turned, the entirety of which may well now be surrounding the van.

"What do we do now?" Caroline asked, her voice both a gasp and a demand. Although trying to take control of the situation and sound like she was keeping it together, she could scarcely breathe and her heart was pounding so hard she could hear it in her ears. "Why is the van not loud enough to keep them away?"

"We're low on gas," Charlie admitted. "The thing is so damned unpredictable. I should have dealt with it when car repair shops were still a thing." He made a mental note to tell Adrian to send a party out to siphon gas from nearby cars.

"Just turn on more music for now," Adrian told him. He pressed play on the box, causing a song Adrian both enjoyed and hated to start playing: the fourth track.

"Have we tried the bug spray *on* the zombies?" Trevor yelled over the music. "It might work on them. Like pepper spray?"

Nobody made a move to test this theory, knowing what would happen if it didn't work. "It couldn't hurt," Raleigh said with a shrug. "We can't just stay in here, assuming they're going to give up on getting to us. After seeing the dead bodies and the zombies on the way here, we're probably the only living things around for miles. I mean, um, aside from your parents, Adrian. It's only a matter of time until they start trying to break the windows or knock the van over."

"You have to roll down a window!" Adrian shouted, knowing that would let the sound waves travel right to the zombies' ears. The music was beyond loud to those in the van, but it wasn't affecting the zombies outside. "Charlie, turn it off for a second." With a nod, Charlie hit the pause button and Adrian took a deep breath. "They're getting stronger. And smarter. It's exactly what I was worried about, and it's happening. You think zombie Nathan would care if I threw some goldfish at him? No! He'd glance at them, then grind them underfoot, not back away. We need to start over: use what we have to find out what repels them in this later state. Charlie, don't turn the music on unless I signal you." She forced her hand to reach for the window button and press "down."

The zombies in Fairborn were equally as aggressive as those in Springfield. Within seconds, grey decomposing hands were clumsily groping for whatever was alive in the van; more hands reaching inside than those prepped to attempt fighting them off. She hated the fact that this was *her* plan and she shouldn't just tell Charlie to turn the music back on, so knowing she couldn't react in the same fashion she did when she'd seen Lucy, Adrian shook off the hand which had grabbed her, resulting in the fingers all breaking off and falling onto her lap as she aimlessly began spraying the bug repellant out the window. The backlash of the spray that went back into her face was uncomfortable, but it wasn't anywhere near as bad as it must have been for the zombies, who suddenly stopped grabbing and retreated not just from the window Adrian was spraying from, but started shuffling off down the street, now significantly weaker than they had been minutes ago, never once looking back. The can of bug spray, now empty, was thrown out the widow as a warning to other zombies who might come along, letting know them that the team was not only expecting them but knew how to get rid of them.

"I don't know why I thought that would be easy," Adrian panted, rolling the window up. "They're either stronger and braver here than in Springfield, or the ones in Springfield are also getting better. At being zombies, that is."

"But you took care of them," Charlie reminded her, rubbing her shoulder. "Now we can safely get out of the van." Adrian shrugged in agreement and pulled the handle on the door, cracking it open. Charlie had pulled the van as close to the front door as he could, but they still had about a twenty foot dash.

"So we're here," Adrian said, turning around in her seat. "We got rid of those ones trying to get in, and there's none around right now." With that, they opened the door of the van and ran to the cement porch.

Adrian's parents lived in a very old house, so the front door was rarely locked. Unfortunately, today it was. Adrian felt a twinge of hope: maybe they were still inside and had never even left the house. Like Charlie earlier, they didn't know what was going on outside.

"It's an old house," Adrian said. "I've got this." After a few seconds of tinkering with the keyhole using a ballpoint pen, Adrian had it unlocked. The small group stepped into the house Adrian had grown up in.

Stepping into the front room, Adrian was suddenly involuntarily struck by memories of the nights she'd spent moving between rooms, trying to find a place she could make herself fall asleep, ultimately ending up in this room watching late night television at a volume low enough that it wouldn't disturb her parents. As she scoured the house, all sense of nostalgia left her. The house was clearly empty. *At least we didn't find any remains,* she thought.

"What do you think this means?" Adrian asked anyone in the room, looking for anything other than her theories: either her parents had left or they'd been forcibly removed from their house. Forcible removal seemed more likely, given that the front door was still locked, but that meant also that they were dead or among the zombies they'd seen roaming the city, maybe even just outside. Neither were very pleasant thoughts.

"It's okay," Charlie told her, gently rubbing her shoulders. "We knew it was an incredibly slim chance that they'd still be here, knowing how independent they both are, but don't let this set you back. For all we know, they went out the back door, which is unlocked, and are still at the picnic. Or, they left early and spent the night at Aunt Gertrude's." He was going to make sure not to check the back door and to leave Adrian assuming that is what must have happened, hoping she'd entertain that idea.

"It's all my fault," Adrian wailed, wrapping her arms around her husband's neck. "We should have warned them, and Karen, and everyone else. And we all know *Hank* could have survived if I stopped him, not to mention—"

"Adrian, darling, breathe for a moment," Charlie coaxed, rubbing small circles on her back. "Hank wasn't right, and there is no way your folks would have believed us if we'd told them. In fact, they would have left their house, gotten into the car and dragged us out of our safe zones to an asylum, claiming we were insane."

He was right, of course. Although Adrian's parents were reasonably accepting of Adrian and her love of zombie books, they were very old-fashioned and would have absolutely gone off on her, had she warned them about what was happening. Next to that, the fact that this was happening in Springfield *as well as* Fairborn did not necessarily mean it was going on wherever her parents had traveled to. Assuming they left the house yesterday.

Adrian was beginning to think that perhaps Charlie was right and her parents had found some place they could be safe.

All of the surviving members of her team had gathered around her. The feeling of community that this created, along with her husband's soothing words, made Adrian feel better and blocked out most of the negative emotions about what might have happened to her folks.

"Okay everyone," Adrian said, allowing them to back off from the embrace, "I'm doing a lot better now."

She explained how important it was to have them all there, comparing her current state of mind with characters in the novels she'd read all throughout her life. It had hurt her earlier when only a small group believed what was happening. But as the day progressed, she came to feel closer with these people than she had ever thought possible, much closer than anyone had in any of the literature she'd so eagerly consumed. The relations she had with some of them had had a rocky start, but now she felt she really knew these people, and she cared about them and that they felt the same. She even felt a special connection to Karl. The thought that he might become infected or bitten truly upset her.

"Do you need some time alone here?" Trevor asked, wondering if they needed to think of something to distract her.

"This is weird, but would you mind if I took you all on a tour of the house?" she asked, a little sheepishly. She thought it might help her leave the house once and for all if she purged some of her negative memories.

In the front room, Adrian talked about how many times she had woken up on the couch, realizing she didn't feel any more rested after sleeping there than she would have in her own bed. It was about a foot too small for her, and she always ended up removing the cushions and putting them on the floor with another cushion added from the couch in the back. She had never fallen into REM sleep using this strategy, but it didn't make a difference, anyway.

She led them into the back room and showed them the couch from which she would get the cushion, which was the correct size for her to sleep on, but never changed a thing. Equally as interesting for everyone involved, the rest of the tour led through the kitchen and dining room, and the one place she was *never* to go: her parents' room.

"And here," she said, opening the door to the one room they hadn't seen. "It always started here. My childhood room."

She turned on the light and heard polite, "Hmmm...." sounds they all made when they saw the hideous pink flowered wallpaper.

"Yeah, I insisted on getting this wallpaper when I was four or five years old, and we never had the money to redecorate it. I didn't realize I was buying little old lady wallpaper. That is one of the many reasons I swore that when I grew up, I was going to work in the news. I knew I'd have money to decorate my place however I wanted. I just had to figure out which part of the news I was going to get a job in."

"And you're *sure* this sleep issue didn't stem from sleeping in the ugliest room in the house," Karl asked, making Adrian laugh a bit.

"Here's what I'm thinking," Adrian said, shutting off the light and turning back to the group, "either my parents are in a bad situation, or safe at the family gathering they planned on going to. In either of those cases, they're not coming back and they don't need any of the things in this house. Let's take what we think will be helpful at the warehouse, then get out of here." It surprised everyone (Adrian included) that she was able to come up with that plan and blow past the possibility that they were dead, but all agreed and immediately went to work looking for things that might help.

It looked like the zombies might have been through, as things were knocked over, missing, or slightly broken. Dishes were on the floors, pillowcases were missing pillows, and the television had been knocked over. The things that *were* left weren't in great condition, but still got grabbed.

It was 7 in the morning by the time they were pleased with everything they had gathered. Still rather dark out though the sky was beginning to lighten up. All of the curtains were drawn, but Charlie took the initiative to look outside and see how they were doing in terms of being alone.

As it happened, the zombies knew they didn't do well around bug spray, as Adrian's leaving the empty can kept them all from getting much closer than five feet in their area. With this discovery, they likely had as much time as they wanted (if not more) to get everything packed into the van. The pile by the front of the door was very tall and filled with things that would be helpful, even if broke: a couple of blankets, some soap, and a few board games and books.

"We should start carrying things out in pairs of two," Trevor decided. "You know, like they always made us do at camp? No one was allowed out alone?"

"We could make these things slightly more compact," Nick observed, his rest having done him quite well. "All these blankets need to be folded, multiple pillows in one pillow case, maybe put some of the food into bags?"

"Good thinking," Adrian agreed, suddenly finding herself giving everyone a task to do and going to get some bags from her parents' storage room. "We might be able to squeeze this into one trip." With Charlie, Karl, Caroline and Raleigh on folding duty, Trevor, Linda, Nick and Denise arranging the food to be put into bags and Adrian retrieving the bags to put the food in, everyone had a job to do.

The team folding sheets was finished first, having simply folded every blanket up into one folded bit of fabric. The food team being a bit more obsessive about keeping the separate types of food apart from each other, and Adrian found they were a little low on bags. They needed two trips, not one, but before they knew it, in the chilly early-morning fall air, the van was packed. Everything now in the van, the ten of them squeezed themselves in among all the blankets, food and various other supplies, fitting now less comfortably than they had before this trip. As many supplies as Charlie had brought from his own house, they now felt they had absolutely everything they could need in any type of issue that might come up; while the original batch of help only included food, bedding of sorts and some medication, they now had electronics, things needed to prepare and eat the food that was brought, and other such necessities. The only thing they could have needed now was more fuel, but their safe house was only a quarter mile away.

"Charlie, dear, you didn't happen to grab a Bible while you were panic loading everything into the van, did you?" Adrian asked, her voice dripping with toxic sweet.

Having been raised Methodist and still attending weekly church services as an adult, Adrian considered herself a woman of faith. What would the Bible have to say about zombies? She was certain there wouldn't be anything under the index of passages about "zombies" or even "the undead", but there had to be something. The closest thing she could think to help would be anything about "soul", which she firmly believed left the body when a person turned. She knew that a human's most primal instinct is to survive, and it couldn't be that different, even if you didn't technically have a soul any longer.

"Should I have?" he asked, his face twisting into a nervous grimace. He had actually packed two different editions; ones he'd seen Adrian reading more than once. There was the mint green one, which was an English Standard Version translation, along with the King James Version one she would go to when she needed an answer, and she needed it fast.

"I can help, if you have more than one," Linda said, having been raised as a religious person herself. She'd lost contact with all of it for a while, but this seemed like the perfect time to get back to it.

"Who's closest to the back?" Charlie said, having thrown most of the books into the back of the van, gently placing the Bibles there as well.

"That would be us," Denise called. Charlie told her what the two books looked like, and she dug around, trying to find them. A few moments later, she came away with them, then passed them up for Adrian and Linda. Charlie knew that his wife hated being in a moving vehicle while she was trying to do research, so he started the engine for noise, but didn't take off yet.

Going to the index at the back of the Bible, Adrian explained her basic idea: look for anything it had to say about the soul, since she believed the soul left when the person died and that it didn't come back when they were a zombie, and what it had to say about death. Linda offered to be the one to look up "dead" and "death", leaving the nicer "soul" passages for Adrian.

The first few passages Adrian read weren't entire helpful, as they spoke of loving the Lord with all of your soul, which she already knew. They didn't say much about what happened if you didn't, but then she found some inspiration from Ezekiel, Matthew, Jeremiah, and 1 Peter. The first message she was able to take from the reading was that maybe the people turning into zombies were sinful, but that didn't really explain those who got attacked by the zombies, and definitely didn't help her process Hank's death any better. She didn't even know who in the company (other than Linda, as she just found out) was religious.

Next, she found help in a passage that clarified what she had just read, talking about those who are following the correct path will go to Heaven once they pass. She still felt that the soul died when the person did, as the zombies all seemed to be completely driven by a primal instinct to survive, so they would be saved.

The more she read, the more she realized each passage basically said the same thing, but made her feel considerably better. If a zombie didn't have a soul, then whatever they did as an undead being didn't hinder whether or not the soul went to Heaven.

As Adrian was collecting all the information she could, Linda was discovering a very similar issue in her search for passages on dead and death: a lot of it was about Jesus coming down and sacrificing himself to save the dead, but did manage to find some inspiration in later passages: there was a specific passage that mentioned how God judges both the living *and* the dead, which was more a question for a philosopher than a newspaper employee, but she liked to think it meant that God judged the living before they came back, undead and only judged it as a corpse before it reanimated. In a more positive passage, it spoke of the Lord "swallowing up death forever", which could mean that this whole thing was going to blow over at some point, but then zombies aren't technically *dead*...

It was refreshing to see a passage mentioning death in a metaphorical sense, as she understood it, talking about those who already died hearing the Good Word. She read it as anybody who wasn't religious should come to be, but she'd never been the kind of person to try and convert others, and she didn't think Adrian would, either.

She read more passages, she came to understand and think that as long as the person had been a believer *before* they turned into a zombie, what they did in their reanimation wouldn't count against them morally. It was well known that zombies didn't have souls, so she didn't understand what they'd all been so worried about to begin with.

308

Ch. 36
The Sweet Smell of Success

Assuming Adrian had all the information she could get at the time, Charlie pulled out of the driveway, leaving the empty bug spray can on the lawn. Nobody spoke, mostly deep in thought about the state of the house that had been fairly empty, but was now stripped of everything that was left, and abandoning the mystery of the whereabouts of Adrian's parents.

"Are we all okay?" Charlie asked from his spot in the front of the van. "Physically, mentally, in terms of still being human?"

"I feel like shit," Trevor muttered. Having been left to his own thoughts as they rummaged through the contents of the house they were just in, it finally came to him that their only real chance at survival was a nuclear explosion of some sort. It was the only way to knock out the zombies and mosquitoes passing the virus, but unless they just happened to stumble upon a bomb shelter, they'd all die, too. All humans would. He'd been alone with these thoughts for a few hours now and he figured it was only a matter of time until it sank in for Adrian and Charlie. He tried to ignore the possibility of it actually happening: whoever dropped the nuclear weapon might possibly survive, *if* they were high enough out of the area of detonation. But then, could death be much worse than what they were going through? He honestly didn't know and wasn't clear headed enough to come up with any type of answer for such a question, wondering if he should be hoping that this ends up happening. There may have been safety in numbers, but their numbers were unreasonably fewer than those already infected and what were a few casualties versus exterminating the new evil in the world?

"I mean, think about it," he blurted, "if the government knows a way to get rid of all those infected but keep some survivors alive, they're not going to do a sweep to figure out who's still alive, right? We'll all die. All of us. And the world's not even going down that fast; there could be thousands, no millions, of people on airplanes from out of the country headed here on vacation who bring even more of the virus over. Or even mutations of it." They hadn't even been in the van for two minutes, and already they were beginning to think everything was futile: by hiding in the safe house, nobody would come to find them and they could all get blown up just as Trevor suggested. Nobody knew what to say, as there was no way to argue with his logic, and agreeing didn't seem like it would be very helpful for anyone.

"We'll take it a day at a time," Linda decided. "Let's not think about those possibilities right now. Hell, for all we know everyone with any government involvement is already dead." After a moment, she mentioned how nobody could even tell if they'd been turned since they were all already mindless beings. Lucy sure as hell hadn't. This observation lightened the mood considerably.

"We're here," Charlie announced, turning off the engine. "We're here and we're out of gas. We made it. Nobody's going to take the van."

"Oh thank *God,*" Denise said, looking at the building they were now parked (if not stranded) in front of. "I'm sorry, but when you guys said an old warehouse, I couldn't help but think you were taking us to one like that one on West Main." She was referring to a totally burned out warehouse in Springfield with absolutely no protection that had almost all of the windows shattered.

"No safety there," Charlie said with a laugh. "Everybody grab something and take it into the warehouse." A feeling of security settled upon Adrian as she started to think that maybe—just maybe—they were going to be okay. The wooded area was really empty, and the looming warehouse looked completely out of place, like someone had created a building, not known what to do with it, and just dropped it into a patch of forest in the middle of the smallest town they could find. There were multiple conspiracies around town that it was a CIA base, or a nuclear testing plant, and other such insane things. Moving here was the best idea any of them had heard in quite a while, and nobody wasted any time grabbing as much as they could possibly carry and start making trips in to settle in.

Less than half an hour later, all the clothes, blankets, electronics and various bits of food were out of the van, in a pile by the front door of the building. This left the mattresses that Charlie had brought, though, knowing that would be a team effort.

"How's everybody doing?" Charlie asked, knowing full well that none of them were doing too well. Cranky and exhausted, they mostly looked at him with disgust, all knowing that if they wanted the rest they so desperately needed, they'd have to help finish unpacking the van. Whispering to only his wife, Charlie asked her again which ones were cooperative and which ones should be left alone, to which she replied Nick was cool but probably needed more rest, to let Karl do whatever the fuck he wanted, and the rest shouldn't be too much of a problem. He asked her to stay by the door and work on figuring out who got how much of what they'd already brought in while he and some of the others started getting the mattresses from the van, after which everyone was going to go to sleep.

"In fact," he said to her, "stay here and we'll set you up a bed immediately. Don't worry about anything else, we'll be right back for you." It was a nice sentiment, but Adrian knew she wouldn't be able to settle any time soon and there would be a ton of noise still going on as they continued hauling the mattresses in.

Either way, Adrian sat, waiting for her husband and some of the others to bring a mattress. "Where do you want it?" Charlie asked her, noting that she didn't look nearly as excited at the prospect of sleep as he'd expected her to be. She shrugged indifferently, almost passive-aggressively, a behavioral factor he had never seen from her. In truth, she had been thinking about it but she couldn't figure out if she'd be more comfortable with a lot of people nearby as she tried to sleep or wanted to be far away from everyone, so she left it to those carrying the mattress to figure it out.

"I want to keep an eye on you," Charlie told her. "But I also want to help everyone get settled in. Can we just leave the mattress here and start getting settled?" She nodded her head, not really comprehending what he was trying to say to her but wanting to be left alone, finally realizing herself just how desperately she needed the sleep she had failed to get in the last couple of hours. She thought about how she could have been down while they drove on the expressway and that she wouldn't have had to see all the changes that had gone on through this event, her mind clouded with the thoughts of all her family and friends looking like the undead they had come across in town. In fact, for all she knew every one of them was somebody that they knew, who she'd grown up with. It could have been the Foy's family, her parents may have been there, all of her school teachers, they may all have been the people who were trying to attack them not fifteen minutes ago.

Even so, Adrian laid down and shut her eyes, her mind still racing at a million miles a second. She could hear as everyone started moving things from the front door and began arranging things to their liking (nobody wanted to set their bed on any floor aside from the first) and did her best to focus just on that, not anything her mind wanted to go to. She thought about her parents and how they probably weren't dead but at another safe place but happened to have forgotten their phones which is why she shouldn't call them to find out if they were okay. She thought about Nathan and how he was not only never going to ridicule her work but also wasn't outside eating the brains and the bodies of any living thing since they'd gotten rid of him. And finally of Hank. Poor Hank, the one she couldn't handle having lost, who was gone for good, never coming back, but ultimately alright. He wouldn't have to put up with any of these feelings that Adrian and everyone else were suffering, and he was probably happy, wherever he was.

Ch. 37
Call Northside 777

Against all odds, Adrain fell asleep rather quickly. Against even bigger odds, she felt pretty well rested when she woke up, hours later the next afternoon. The first thing she did was go find Charlie to make sure he was alright.

Everything had been unpacked and put away, she noticed, which meant Charlie had put everyone to work. She searched the entire layout of the first floor, finding a bed in almost every room, some of them with people sleeping, some with messed up sheets meaning she wasn't the only one who had slept and gotten up. After a short time, she went to the second floor, where she found Charlie messing with door of an empty cabinet. She cleared her throat and entered the room, trying not to startle him too badly.

"You're up!" he exclaimed. "Were you ever down..."

"Oddly, yes," Adrian told him. "How's everyone doing?" Charlie extracted himself from whatever activity he'd been in the middle of doing and led her out of what was now the kitchen. They began walking around the second floor, Charlie showing her where everything was and telling her what he knew.

"So there's really nobody keeping a bed up here," Charlie let her know, "but we decided this floor would be used mostly for storage and recreation. And we figured sometimes we'll need to be away from each other, which is what this room is for." They had entered a room that was not bare walled like all of the others, but instead had crude drawings of the sun and smiley faces done with cement. It felt like a power play either by Raleigh or Karl.

"I approve," she said with a nod. "In fact, I think I want to stay in this room for just a little while longer."

"Do you want me to stay with you, or..." Adrian nodded; having spent the entire past day knowing he might have turned or gotten attacked, she wasn't going to let Charlie out of her sight at any time soon. She sat cross-legged on the gritty floor, taking in all of the happy pictures and stopping her mind from adding the image of zombies to them. Charlie sat next to her and put an arm around her shoulder.

"We're all okay," he whispered into her hair. "I've been keeping an extra close eye on everyone, and all they've been doing is settling in. I think they're going to stay away from us for a bit."

"Do they hate me that much now?" she whispered as silently as she could. There was nobody on the same floor as them and everyone else in the building was asleep, but Adrian didn't want anybody knowing how scared she still was.

"I think Aster secretly really enjoyed everything that happened yesterday," Charlie told her, laughing to himself. That seemed odd to her: after all the judgement and mistreatment Karl given her, it didn't seem like that would be true. But maybe all he needed was some sleep. And Caroline. Caroline clearly helped. Then again, she'd only met the guy yesterday...

"What else?" Adrian said, getting up from the floor. "What else has been set up?" The rest of the tour was fairly dull: the other rooms were still rather empty but each had a certain activity that was to be done in each of them, and downstairs again was just everyone's bedroom.

"So this is home now, huh?" Adrian said after the tour had ended and she knew everyone was all settled in.

"Looks like it," Charlie told her as the two stood and surveyed the room: Caroline was resting while Karl watched on to make sure nobody disturbed her, Raleigh was talking animatedly with Nancy about something that might have been wedding plans (Adrian figured, as Natalie was standing close by), Trevor and Linda had been sent off on a task of designating an area in the wood that everyone would use as a bathroom, and Denise was busy fussing over making sure that now that Nick was asleep, he couldn't roll over onto his injured wrist.

"Everyone's got their own space, no one is about to come all the way out here to try to find refuge from whatever's going on, we've got the repellant, and nobody here is going to turn." Their weird little band of survivors seemed to be doing fine, but Adrian herself was a complete and total mess. She knew they were perfectly safe and that they could do away with any zombies that might come to find them, but after what they'd just had to go through, she couldn't calm down. There was an everlasting feeling in the pit of her stomach that something was about to happen, that nothing was ever going to feel the same again, and she knew nothing was ever going to go back to normal. Even if this whole thing worked itself out, the amount of PTSD, the economic status of the world, and the amount of jobs lost and buildings that needed repair would skyrocket.

What they had just gone through was a completely different experience for each person who had lived a completely different life, but the impact it would have on the world would all be the same. For Adrian herself, she was in charge for the first time and with higher stakes than she would have ever wanted her to have to take care of. She hoped it would never come to that again. As things had started to look out of the ordinary that morning, she assumed her boss would have taken care of it, never knowing she would be their only real chance at

surviving through the night.
And maybe for the rest of their lives.

Epilogue

"I miss alcohol," Adrian said, scowling at the contents of her mug. They were throwing an official engagement for Nancy and Natalie, but it could have been more fun.

Linda agreed, looking at what remained in her mug, and swirling the liquid. All she had left was a weakly flavored mock juice and leftover clumps of what had flavored it. In the real world, it was a weight loss substance, but here they used it sparingly at celebrations.

"How much of this junk do we have left, anyway?" Karl asked, squinting into his cup. It had a strange effect on people, as it was not only for weight loss but also loaded with caffeine: it caused tingles all up and down their bodies. Karl didn't love the sensation, but at the same time, he had to admit he didn't hate it. It reminded him that he was still alive.

"Not the current focus," Adrian said, snapping out of the conversation. They had all gathered to celebrate an engagement, not complain about running out of admittedly bad juice.

"Hey gang," Natalie said, joining the group, "what are we all talking about?" In Adrian's head, she pictured each and every member of the circle blurting out a

different topic, but instead she admitted, "We were
discussing how... different things have become. But that's
nowhere near as interesting or different as you and Nancy
finally planning on tying the knot. How does it feel?"
Natalie giggled.
"I can't even complain that this is the
circumstance," she admitted. "Think about it: no matter
what, we'll be spending the rest of our lives together. And
I absolutely *love* the idea of Charlie officiating. It's so us.
Unconventional."
When they all had gotten to the bunker, it sunk in
for the two women that they wouldn't ever be able to get
officially married. Once it had become clear that this was
their new reality, the couple wanted to do anything in
their power to get married. Even though it was nothing
official, Charlie pointed out that he was, more or less, a
captain, and captains were able to officiate weddings, as
seen in classic *Trek* episode "Balance of Terror".
Adrian had to confess that the two women were
definitely cute together, and neither were particularly
unattractive. Although they both had vastly different
appearances, they were both very beautiful.
Everyone stood around wearing the closest thing
each had to nice clothing and all were gathered to
congratulate the two women. They'd been in the safe
house for just over a week, but they were all starting to
take note of things they'd need to learn to live without.
Each couple settled into a routine, having their specific
job to be done a regular basis.
Any time there didn't sound to be much
disturbance outside, a few of the braver members (a
category that changed almost daily) would venture into
the woods to pick some of the berries that they, through
trial and error, had discovered were safe to eat.
While they hadn't been there for long, each of

them had changed profoundly: for one, now everybody was a vegetarian, as they couldn't eat any of the infected animals that would actually be quite easy to hunt and kill, Nick and Denise had taught everyone how to use basic kitchen aids to sanitize, and Karl's ADHD tendencies seemed to be rubbing off on everybody. Only one thing had stayed the same: Charlie was always there any time Adrian got overwhelmed.

As the party began to wear down, Nick offered the most Nick thing ever: in order to ignore what was happening right outside, he could easily begin a Dungeons and Dragons campaign. "I mean, we'd definitely not have zombies in this particular campaign, but it'd be fun," he explained. He'd been a Dungeon Master for enough years that he wouldn't struggle to help make character sheets for everybody who wanted to join in. It wouldn't be easy, per se, but he could explain the basic races and classes to whoever wanted to join, and more or less start over on the campaign he'd just been working.

The first to jump in was Scott, who (although he was happy for his twin sister) really didn't want to celebrate her engagement with his ex-girlfriend. Slowly but surely, others sat with the two on the floor, until 5 people had broken down and joined, leaving them with enough people for an interesting and fun game. Each person who had joined had had very different lives, and Nick had a feeling that each person would create their own character based on it.

A few hours later, each person had made his or her own character, some very similar to what his or her own personality was, or almost the exact opposite.

Adrian stood, watching the different activities of her new little family, proud to see they'd all made it this far. She couldn't believe that a group of coworkers from a newspaper would be getting along this well, sitting together and playing a role playing game. She loved it.

Dusk was upon them by this point, and Adrian wanted to gather some of the sweeter berries as a nice treat for everybody. She had to do it before it got too dark, so she let Charlie (who apparently was now "Holg") know she was going outside. They'd forgone the concept of "the buddy system" they'd used for the first couple days, as it was weird any time they were going out to relieve themselves, and had all agreed to just let somebody know before they left.

As he watched his wife leave the safety of the decrepit building, Charlie realized she was becoming really depressed about something. Something was wrong with her, and it wasn't that she'd become a zombie. She never offered to go get extra snacks unless she needed to be alone and parse something out for herself.

He wished he could do something about it, but now that they had Raleigh with them, Adrian suddenly decided that she wouldn't discuss anything unless it was with a licensed professional. Their licensed professional was currently rolling for hit points, so not going to be much help.

"Natural twenty," Raleigh announced.

Adrian had adapted pretty well to living in their bunker, but didn't think she'd ever get used to their bathroom situation. The first day of the apocalypse, when they were still in the news building, they had the option every now and then to go down the hall and use the restroom. They did not have that luxury any longer, and were stuck doing what they needed to do a few feet away from the building in a particularly bushy area.

Either way, Adrian held onto a tree and crouched down. As she urinated, she took a moment to think about how much more difficult this was for her as a woman than it was for the men.

Before she had too much time to ruminate this complaint, realized what she'd been staring at for the past five seconds: a mosquito. It hadn't processed in her brain that that's what it was, as it was three inches long.

"Fuck."

Acknowledgments

Starting and finishing a novel is a lot of work, and I couldn't have done what I did by myself. From being brought up with a love of the written word to college professors being incredibly good at their job, I was able to write this book.

Firstly, I would like to thank my mother, who had a firm belief that a sick day from school was the best and only possible time to work on my writing skills. I handed in some kick ass essays back in the day, never considering that I might be obtaining a type of knowledge that would help me in my career. But at least I was never bored.

Similarly, I want to thank my dad, who was there when I randomly spouted off every detail of what I would write if I ever wrote a zombie book. It was completely theoretical and I never thought it would happen, but he didn't tell me it was a bad idea, which I might have taken a bit far now that I think about it. But I took the challenge.

In terms of actually sitting down and bringing this book to completion, I have two people who deserve all of the credit. To my best friend during my final semester of college, Ally, you read the first draft before it was even finished, before anybody but Hank had been fleshed out, and somehow actually enjoyed the experience. At the time, working on the book was just a way of distracting myself from the upcoming doom of presenting my senior research (which was essentially just an excuse to talk about various fandoms in front of the English department) and I didn't think anything would ever come of it. Knowing you liked it, though, I took it upon myself to not only finish the draft, but polish it so it could be published. I owe you so much.

While Ally is the reason I wanted to get serious about getting my book to actual humans, Judy Hersch is the reason that it actually happened. I was in a really dark place when I decided to get published (and no, I don't mean Springfield), but over the course of about a year, she helped me figure out that I was meant to write this book, and I wasn't just convincing myself that it was something that needed to be done. She helped me through getting it written to completion, thinking about why I wanted to write it, and was always supportive regardless of what stage of writing I was in.

Judy was the reason I went ahead and published my novel, but along the way I also got a lot of help from my writing coach, Marcy Pusey. At some point along the way, I started questioning if writing truly was the thing I should be doing, or if I was simply doing it as a hobby. Time and time again, though, Marcy told me that she could tell I was meant to be a writer. Hearing that from someone you respect so much just means everything, and it really got me to be even more serious. I reached milestones and did things in my writing because of her support.

They say "don't judge a book by its cover". I have never truly agreed with this statement, and now that I've written a book, I know just how false a statement that is. I need to thank everybody at Cutting Edge Studios for the work that they do, specifically my cover designer, Marijke. You got me from an incredibly specific design I thought I wanted to a more comic and plot driven picture that I absolutely love. I never felt nervous about asking for updates, and you took my every point into account. Even my obsessive font choices.

At the risk of sounding cliché, I would like to name a few teachers who helped form me into the writer that I am today.

Professor Beth Myers, your creative writing classes really got me to understand that what I had been writing was the most basic skeleton of a zombie novel. You gave us an assignment one day in which we were supposed to take a character we'd written and give them a scar. I obviously chose Hank, and you convinced me to push it further and give him brain damage on top of the scar. Which turned him into arguably the most fleshed out character I've ever written, and got me to give everybody in my book a backstory other than "this person likes or doesn't like this thing".

Professor Collins, I think we both knew I wasn't going to grow up to work in the journalism industry. But you were super cool, we bonded over a mutual love of Star Trek, and I didn't want everything I learned in your classes to go to the wayside. You were always really supportive, even when I didn't exactly excel at the subject.

And finally, my Freshman English teacher, as well as (I wanna say?) English 304, or Joseph Campbell's Hero Journey Through *Harry Potter*. I took what I learned in that class to flesh out this book, then wrote the words around it. I'd had this idea for a zombie novel, but what I learned in that class really helped me make this thing happen. Also, you were never easy on Freshman Lisa, who didn't exactly realize college writing and high school writing were two completely different things.

Then there was this one guy I met at con once, who somehow inspired me. I saw him, and that night, I became really motivated to see my novel to completion. So, to the random guy, thank you.

ABOUT THE AUTHOR

Pictured with rat, Adrian. Not pictured: Hank, Nick, and Charlie.

Lisa Fedel hates talking about herself, and in fact found writing her author bio synonymous to setting up a dating profile. When she must, however, she chooses to use the funnel method, which is the most fun way to write essays. She is a font fanatic (Comic Sans FTW) with a traumatic brain injury and an interest in everything serial killer and cryptid (hey, they tell you to "write what you know"). She became an author purely out of spite to prove she could do it. For reasons far beyond her comprehension, while writing her zombie novel, she decided to go vegan. She has been to Springfield, Ohio once.

We all do exactly what cute dogs tell us to do, right? Ginny here would love any and all positive feedback on this book. Hit me up on Twitter or Facebook.

She also wouldn't hate if you left a review on Amazon.

Thank you!
Lisa Fedel
[transcribed from Ginny's barks and whines]

Made in the USA
Middletown, DE
04 September 2022

72266948R00189